BARBARO
★ AMERICA'S HORSE ★

BARBARO
★ AMERICA'S HORSE ★

Shelley Fraser Mickle

ALADDIN PAPERBACKS
NEW YORK   LONDON   TORONTO   SYDNEY

★ ★ ★

A portion of this book's proceeds is being donated to
the Belmont Child Care Association and the riding camp
at the Kennett Square YMCA.

★ ★ ★

ALADDIN PAPERBACKS

An imprint of Simon & Schuster Children's Publishing Division

1230 Avenue of the Americas, New York, NY 10020

Copyright © 2007 by Shelley Mickle

Designed by Lisa Vega

The text of this book was set in Centaur MT.

Manufactured in the United States of America

First Aladdin Paperbacks edition March 2007

2 4 6 8 10 9 7 5 3 1

Library of Congress Cataloging-in-Publication Data

Mickle, Shelley.

Barbaro : America's horse / by Shelley Mickle.—1st Aladdin Paperbacks ed.

p. cm.

ISBN-13: 978-1-4169-4865-0 (pbk)   ISBN-10: 1-4169-4865-1 (pbk)

ISBN-13: 978-1-4169-4866-7 (library)   ISBN-10: 1-4169-4866-X (library)

1. Barbaro (Race horse)—Juvenile literature.

2. Race horses—United States—Biography—Juvenile literature. I. Title.

SF355.B37M53 2007

636.1'2—dc22   2007000678

Barbaro

ON JANUARY 29, 2007, BARBARO'S owners, Gretchen and Roy Jackson, were forced to make the painful decision to put down their beloved horse, who had fought valiantly for nearly a year with an injury so great, almost no one believed he'd survive for so long. The odds had finally caught up with this brave animal.

The world mourned Barbaro's death, especially his owners and the caretakers who had lovingly tended him from birth, through his training and brilliant racing career, and through his heroic battle against his devastating injury. But the example Barbaro left for all of us—the courage and grace with which he fought adversity and faced uncertainty—are here for all time. He is a champion for the ages.

★ ★ ★ ★ ★ ★ ★ ★ ★ ★ ★ ★

Author's Note

BARBARO: AMERICA'S HORSE IS A faithful depiction of the life of this extraordinary horse. To make the story come alive to young readers, I have fleshed out the facts with fictionalized details, such as thoughts and conversations of people close to Barbaro, all based on my interviews with them. I have also attempted to get inside the head and heart of Barbaro himself to help the reader understand fully his remarkable spirit and his inspiring story.

★ ★ ★ ★ ★ ★ ★ ★ ★ ★ ★ ★

Contents

★ ★ ★ ★ ★ ★ ★ ★ ★ ★ ★ ★

★ ★ ★ ★ ★ ★ ★ ★ ★ ★ ★ ★

★ ★ ★ ★ ★ ★ ★ ★ ★ ★ ★ ★ ★ ★ ★

Introduction

WINNING THE KENTUCKY DERBY WITH
our homebred Barbaro was one of the most
exciting days of our lives. We were thrilled,
and it seemed he captured the hearts of
many racing fans as well as newcomers to
the sport. Delighted by the response, we
realized we could share him with his fans.
Our beloved Barbaro was now America's
horse.

But as quickly as that euphoric moment
transformed our lives, we were brought up
short by the unexpected injury at the start
of the Preakness. Nothing can describe our
family's pain, and nothing can remove the
memory. However, something happened
that was more powerful than that tragic
moment on the Pimlico track.

In an instant (or so it seemed), Barbaro
and all his caretakers were surrounded by

★ ★ ★ ★ ★ ★ ★ ★ ★ ★ ★ ★ ★

loving support from his fans. As the ambulance trailer made its way from Pimlico to New Bolton Center, people placed banners on the overpasses, declaring their support and sharing their prayers. People gathered at New Bolton's gates with signs that were illuminated by the headlights of the truck pulling Barbaro's trailer.

With this indescribable flood of well-wishing, prayers, and support, Barbaro entered his time of healing, and, I might say, so did we. In the following days, weeks, and months an enormous flow of love came to us in letters, cards, signs, flowers, fruit baskets, horse snacks, religious medals, books, and stuffed animals. Many, many of these things were from children. All were so very touching and very much appreciated. We, Barbaro's owners and caretakers, cannot express our immense gratefulness for all the outpouring of love and generosity. It made all the difference to us who lived daily with Barbaro and had to make some hard decisions.

Thank you, thank you, thank you. We love you.

Gretchen and Roy Jackson

★ ★ ★ ★ ★ ★ ★ ★ ★ ★ ★ ★ ★ ★

★ CHAPTER 1 ★

The Third Saturday in May

NO ONE WHO SAW IT WOULD EVER forget it. It was the third Saturday in May. The bay colt, dark reddish brown with a white heart on his forehead, stood in the starting gate. He was one of the most famous athletes in America. Everyone expected him to win this race. It seemed there were TV cameras everywhere. The grandstand was filled with thousands of people. Only a moment before, all of them had been talking, sounding like a meeting of bees. But now a hush hung over everything—the grandstand, the racetrack, even the stables farther away. The air crackled with excitement.

Halfway down the line in the starting gate, the young horse could hear the clang and snap of the other horses' gates closing

★ ★ ★ ★ ★ ★ ★ ★ ★ ★ ★ ★

them in. His body was coiling. His legs seemed lit with fire. In only a second now the starting bell would ring, and he would uncoil in a fierce leap forward. He was so eager to run that his legs almost trembled, itching to be let go. He could hear the rhythm of his speed song building, building, building. And then, he could no longer wait.

He burst through the starting gate and ran down the track—alone! The fans in the grandstand gasped.

Another horse, ridden by an outrider, galloped after him to try to catch him and bring him back. Edgar Prado, the young horse's jockey, stood in the stirrups, working hard to tell the horse through the reins, *Look, kiddo, you've jumped the gun. This is not the race yet. Whoa!*

But the young stallion's passion to run was like a fire licking at the ground. His legs sang to their own rhythm: *Run, run. This is what you were born to do. Your whole heart, your hooves, your legs, your lungs say, Run. Run. Run!*

He wanted to never stop.

Only after great effort was the jockey able to pull the horse up and tell him through the reins and the way he changed his weight in the saddle, *Now, come on, we have to go back and do it all over again. Don't fuss. This time wait until I tell you to go!*

The fans in the grandstand murmured. The horse's

trainer worried too. Had the young, eager horse spent too much energy breaking out of the starting gate? Would he be too tired to win the race now?

All eyes watched as the young stallion was led back. The track's veterinarian looked him over, found no injuries, and declared him sound to run. Once again he was led into his place in the starting gate. Prado stroked his neck, speaking calming words. And then the starting bell rang with a loud BRRRR! And the gate sprang open.

The young horse covered the first yards of track as though he were lifting up and soaring over the length of it. "Look. No. He's got plenty of run left," someone in the grandstand said. "The false start isn't going to hurt him a bit. He's *so* strong."

Others now looked for the young stallion's wings to sprout. It seemed he had to have them. He had run six races and won them all—and most of them easily, far out in front of every other horse. He was bound to make history. He would be the most successful racehorse since Secretariat, who had won all three of the most difficult races by many lengths. And that was thirty years before. Everyone thought the bay colt might be the next Triple Crown winner too, since he'd already won the Kentucky Derby and was favored here in the Preakness. He'd have only the Belmont to win next—and the crown would be his!

★ ★ ★ ★ ★ ★ ★ ★ ★ ★ ★ ★ ★

Not everyone expected that Barbaro could do this. From the time he was born, many said he could run fast only on grass. It was said he might never learn how to win races on dirt.

"He lifts his knees too high," some said.

"His running style is more suitable for grass," others pointed out.

"He takes too many vacations," others said. "He's not tough enough for these big races."

But the young horse had proven them all wrong.

His mother could run fast on dirt; his father had been *fast*, period. And they, as well as all the other winners in his family, had passed on to him his ferocious desire to be out front, to be leading the herd, to be running as though his very blood were a fire no one could put out.

"Go, go, go, Barbaro!" the fans were yelling. The sound was deafening during the first few yards of the race.

And then a sudden loud sound of everyone gasping again filled the air.

The young, proud horse had unexpectedly taken a wrong step. His back ankle turned. It was clear his pain was searing, but he did not want to stop. His right hind foot refused to support his weight. The bones in his leg were broken, but he would not let that keep him from running the race.

★ ★ ★ ★ ★ ★ ★ ★ ★ ★ ★ ★ ★ ★

He hobbled; he lunged; he hopped.

He would run, no matter what. He would run until someone fought him to stop. He ran until his jockey jumped off to hold his reins. He shook his broken leg, trying to rid himself of the pain. If he could, he would outrun even the ambulance coming to take him off the track. And then he dipped his head toward his jockey as though to say, *Help me out, here.*

Even as the race ended and another horse won, he ran in his mind, and he ran in his heart.

The crowd watched the ambulance drive away. It was all they could see now of Barbaro. Inside, the young horse concentrated on the pain. He did not yet know he would have to learn how to run in another way.

This time there would be no money prizes. There would be no chance for a line in a racing history book. This time he would run for his life.

★ ★ ★ ★ ★ ★ ★ ★ ★ ★ ★ ★ ★

CHAPTER 2

A Magic Moment

THREE YEARS BEFORE, IN KENTUCKY, on a cool evening on the twenty-ninth of April, a dark brown foal followed the curve of its mother's womb and slid partway out onto the soft stall bedding. Its mother turned her head to look at her baby.

It is always a magic moment when a horse is born.

The foal's hips and back feet were still inside its mother. The farm manager, Bill Sanborn, stepped forward to help. The mare had given birth to only one other foal before. And this was clearly going to be a very big foal.

Bill grabbed the foal's front legs. His wife and the night watchman held its head and shoulders. And when the mare's

★ ★ ★ ★ ★ ★ ★ ★ ★ ★ ★

muscles squeezed again, pushing the foal out, Bill pulled. Soon the foal lay on the straw. Its eyes were closed. Its mouth was like a little fist, held tight.

The mare's name, La Ville Rouge, was French. In English these words mean "red city," but anyone who looked at her could see she was more majestic than her name would suggest. She was a singular, strong, tall horse with a rich brown coat that could smell as good as a baking cake.

She was a good mother, who was now looking at her foal, as if saying, *Is it here? Is it okay? What do you think, huh? Is it as beautiful as I promised?*

Those watching stood still. They moved back against the wall of the stall. Bill Sanborn turned out the lights. In these first few minutes it is important to respect the mother's bond with her baby. The light in the aisle of the barn threw a soft golden glow over the foal.

As always at the birth of any foal, whispers of excitement trickled through the air: "Is it a girl horse? Is it a filly?"

"Is it a male horse? Is it a colt? Can anyone tell yet?"

"Colt," Bill Sanborn whispered. And they all smiled.

The foal was indeed a colt, and a fine one. When he was grown, he would be called a stallion. But today he was La Ville Rouge's colt, small and wet.

The baby quickly propped himself up on his chest,

★ ★ ★ ★ ★ ★ ★ ★ ★ ★ ★ ★ ★ ★

or sternum, and whinnied. He shook his head and snorted. This was nature's way of clearing his nose.

In his first few breaths, hairlike tiny fingers, called cilia, beat inside his lungs and up his airways. They were sweeping the passages clear so he could breathe easily.

He shimmied around to the side of his mother, and as he did, the cord between them broke. For eleven months that cord had kept him alive. It had brought him everything he'd needed to grow so he could then be born. And now the moment had come when it was no longer needed. It dangled from each of them, broken.

The mother horse and her baby were forever separate now.

Everyone was so silent and still in the stall, the moment was almost like a prayer. Yet all were thinking, *Will this colt carry the talent for racing of his famous sire, Dynaformer?*

Just the name of the colt's father, Dynaformer, carried the awe of a great horse. And this colt already wore the bay color of his father. That was apparent even under his wiry foal coat.

But what about all the other qualities a horse has to possess to be a great racehorse? Would he have endurance? Would he be able to run fast for long distances? Would he be trainable? Would he learn his lessons easily? Would he have deep lungs? Would he have the heart to challenge the wind and come in first?

★ ★ ★ ★ ★ ★ ★ ★ ★ ★ ★ ★ ★ ★

Everyone waited for the baby to stand up and nurse. The colt shivered. This was a good sign. It showed that in his brain his weather channel, or thermostat, was working. This was nature's way of telling him to use his muscles to warm up.

He stuck his tongue out and made a sucking noise. His mother nickered and licked him. Then she began biting him, urging him to stand up. She had to get her foal up, quick. If she were in a wild herd on the prairie, and bobcats or wolves were hunting the horses for their dinner, her baby would need to be ready to run. Horses are prey animals—which means others hunt them for food—and they have one main answer to this danger.

Sure, they can kick and bite. But those defenses are nothing compared to being as swift as a moonbeam shimmering across a wild prairie. Running was deep inside the mare's mind. And she was now passing on that message to her baby.

Being in a warm stall in a nice barn didn't take away her instincts. Thousands of years of horses being on earth had planted those behaviors deep in her brain.

The colt struggled to his feet. His legs were as long as hoe handles and as wobbly as spaghetti. He fell once, twice, and then got up again.

Falling was a good thing. It slapped more fluid from his lungs. Nature had planned this, too. He nudged

★ ★ ★ ★ ★ ★ ★ ★ ★ ★ ★ ★ ★

his mother, instinctively knowing exactly what he was looking for. He just had to find it. Where, oh where, was it?

He sucked the air. He sucked the wall. He sucked his mother's hip. He sucked her shoulder. And then she nudged him. *There, there. Yes, a little farther now.* On her underside, he found her udder. And soon warm milk streamed into his mouth.

The milk dribbled down his chin. He glanced at the humans huddled in the corner whispering. Their language sounded strange. But his mother seemed calm, so he wasn't scared.

In time a few of the two-footed creatures' words would begin to make sense to him. He would also learn to read what they said by the way they moved. And he would speak to them in his language—neighs and whinnies and squeals—and with *his* movements.

In time they would all learn to speak to one another in a common language they would build together.

But for now the colt and humans merely looked at one another. They did not yet know of the great things they would accomplish together, nor of the long journey they would travel with one another. And then Bill Sanborn stepped forward and touched the colt.

"Oh, now, aren't you a beauty? You're a big strong

one, aren't you? I bet you'll run like the wind."

Yet the promise of what the bay colt would become lay hidden. It was as unseen as the cricket, singing through the night in a corner of the barn.

★ ★ ★ ★ ★ ★ ★ ★ ★ ★ ★ ★ ★ ★ ★

CHAPTER 3

There's Nothing Like a Good Pair of Genes

ALREADY HE WAS SPECIAL. THE BAY colt carried valuable genes. Genes are what make us who we are. And Barbaro's genes were giving him traits and abilities that all his family members had had before him.

Unlike blue jeans, the genes we inherit don't wear out. They don't get tight or fade in the wash, either. And every creature, no matter who, is able to pass them on.

Barbaro now carried a part of all who had gone before him.

Every cell in his body, every tiny part of him, was carrying two sets of instructions, written in their own language. These messages of life are called DNA.

★ ★ ★ ★ ★ ★ ★ ★ ★ ★ ★

DNA is shaped like a rope and is made up of chemicals. We all have it. Everything on us has it—our hair, our skin, even the tiniest part of us.

One rope of DNA comes from the mother, one from the father. The ropes twist together and carry instructions on structures called chromosomes, which act like ink pens, writing on every part of us. And it is here—in the chromosomes—where thousands of genes live. And they were telling Barbaro how to resemble his mother, his father, his grandparents—all the way back for many generations. Sometimes they were instructing him how to be different.

His chromosomes were telling him to be the warm fudge color of a bay, to have a long strong neck, to be tall, and to have a calm disposition, like a leaf floating on a stream. And they were telling him to have an intelligence as sharp as a sickle blade cutting through weeds. Yes, even Barbaro's personality was designed by his genes.

And no other horse on the whole earth could ever be Barbaro. No one else could ever carry his genes.

Horse breeders called him an outcross. His mother's line had never before been mated with his father's line. He was bringing a new family to the Thoroughbred world. And since nearly two million Thoroughbred horses have all come from the same three stallions, Barbaro was more than valuable. He was going to invigorate, or bring new

★ ★ ★ ★ ★ ★ ★ ★ ★ ★ ★ ★ ★ ★

possibilities to, the Thoroughbred bloodline.

You'd have to say "great" more than twelve times before the word "grandfather" in order to go back to the first three stallions that all Thoroughbreds call their long-ago grandfathers: the Darley Arabian, the Godolphin Arabian, and the Byerly Turk. Three hundred years ago these three horses from the Middle East, who could run fast and long in the desert, were taken to England. There they were bred with stronger horses, so that the breeders could cross the Middle Eastern horses' traits of speed and endurance with strength. Each of these stallions was named for its owner—Thomas Darley, Lord Godolphin, and Captain Robert Byerly.

Since Thoroughbred breeders have only three ancestors or family lines from which to breed generations of racehorses, Thoroughbred horsemen made an important rule. They decided to allow only natural mating between stallions and mares. This limits the number of mares that can have babies from one stallion—after all, bringing a mare to a stallion is much more difficult and time-consuming than merely shipping frozen seed or sperm to another farm. With the natural mating rule, a Thoroughbred stallion can pass his genes to no more than about one hundred and fifty mares a year, reducing the risk of passing along weak or disease-carrying genes through too much in-breeding. This

★ ★ ★ ★ ★ ★ ★ ★ ★ ★ ★ ★ ★ ★

way, the breed stays vigorous and exciting. One never knows when an exceptional horse may come along, an extraordinary athlete like Barbaro.

And now Barbaro was a part of all of this past. Only an hour old, he stood by his mother and felt for the first time the touch of a man's hand on his wiry foal coat. It felt good, and there was nothing to worry about when the two-legged creature, this thing called a man, held his hooves. He then felt the man pat his neck and back and face. Another person cleaned his ears and nose. Soon someone turned out the lights again and everyone tiptoed away and left the mare and her foal together, alone.

Barbaro nursed off and on all night and slept by his mother. The next morning, when rays of sun came through the barn window, he could see his new world clearly. The barn ceiling was tall, and the place smelled like hay and straw and warm milk. He heard the stall door open and saw the man who had helped bring him into the world walk into the stall. The man was speaking softly, "Hey there, my pretty. Welcome to the world. I have a halter here for you to wear. Put your head down just a little. That's right. That's right. Oh, yes, you are good little guy."

Bill Sanborn slipped a tiny halter over the colt's nose and buckled it over his ears. He clipped a rope onto the mother's halter and began to lead her outside.

Barbaro, seeing his mother leave, was alarmed and

★ ★ ★ ★ ★ ★ ★ ★ ★ ★ ★ ★ ★ ★

scampered to keep up. He trotted along beside her as the man led her out into the daylight. From here, in the early morning light, the Kentucky pasture looked blue. The grass seemed to be lightly brushed with a color to match the sky.

From these early moments Barbaro would always remember he had nothing to fear here. Yes, people might look strange—with only two legs, and ears that wouldn't bend, so he couldn't read their moods by the way their ears went backward or forward. But still, people were clearly his friends. They would always help take care of him.

Bill Sanborn opened the gate to a paddock and led in Barbaro's mother, and Barbaro trotted beside her. Another horse and foal were already there. The foal, named Last Best Place, was a chestnut, which meant his coat was the brownish red color of a pine needle. Small and tough, he was as spunky as a prizefighter. He acted as though he were ready to climb into a ring and knock somebody down. He trotted over and touched noses with Barbaro. Curiously, Barbaro reached out and touched noses with *him*.

They both smelled of mare milk. And their coats, though different colors, were wiry and curly. Barbaro had white on each of his front feet and a smidgen of white above his back right foot. And on his nose, as if the heart on his forehead had dripped paint, was a pink snip similar to the shape of a continent on a map of the world.

★ ★ ★ ★ ★ ★ ★ ★ ★ ★ ★ ★ ★ ★

The red colt twitched his ears. He reared and bit Barbaro. He scampered away, kicking grass into Barbaro's face. He then looked back as if he were saying, *How do you like that, big guy? You think you're hot stuff. We'll see. Bet you can't keep up with me.*

Barbaro sniffed the air. He put his head way up and blew a puff of air from his nostrils. The air streamed out white in the cold morning. His mother already had her head down, eating the rich grass, biting it in mouthfuls. After a quick look around, Barbaro bucked. He lifted his back into an arch and popped the air with his back legs. It was as if he were saying, *Oh, yeah? Watch this. I might be only half a day old, but I got the right stuff.* And he took off, scampering the best he could on long legs that were like boat oars— and sometimes just as awkward—slapping the air, rowing him along.

A short time later both colts were lying in the tall grass beside their mothers, tuckered out. Their heads were flat on the ground, their eyes closed, their short tails flicking at flies. Sleeping soundly with the sun warming their fuzzy coats, they were dreaming of milk and remembering the first feel of a wonderful discovery. Oh yes, there was no doubt. They might have been sleeping, but their hearts were awake to the love of speed.

★ ★ ★ ★ ★ ★ ★ ★ ★ ★ ★ ★ ★ ★

★ **CHAPTER 4** ★

Who Says You Can't Falter with a Halter?

WHEN BARBARO WAS SIX WEEKS OLD, a car drove up to the Kentucky farm where he was born. A man and a woman got out and walked over to the pasture fence to look at him. Barbaro now spent every day in a big pasture with five other colts and their mothers.

Gretchen Jackson put on her glasses to see more closely the foal that belonged to her mare La Ville Rouge. Gretchen's glasses, big round circles that covered most of her small face, came down almost to the smile tracks left from many smiles. Her silver hair was the color of a new quarter.

While she studied her foal, her

★ ★ ★ ★ ★ ★ ★ ★ ★ ★

husband, Roy, put his hands on the top fence rail and leaned forward. A big man, as wide and strong as a football player, he had a gentle voice, soft, like a radio turned on low. "Big, isn't he?" Roy said.

"Yes," Gretchen answered, "*very* big. Very nice, too. Look at him, all parts and more parts. Big sloping shoulders, long legs. A nice eye—soft and intelligent. I've been excited to see what this mare would have. I think this colt looks very promising."

"What are you going to name him?" Roy asked.

"I haven't decided yet. I wanted to see him first. Clearly he deserves a special name. When I hear the right one for him, I'll know it. But for now he's just La Ville's colt."

Bill Sanborn came to stand beside them. "Look at that little guy out there with him." He laughed and pointed to the chestnut colt, Last Best Place. "That one's always trying to rule the roost. He reminds me of a tough guy in the movies. But your La Ville colt won't take anything off of him. They tussle every day."

"And how does our colt come out?" Roy wanted to know. As a man who owned baseball teams and helped to manage players, he knew an athlete had to have a desire to win, or physical strength and prowess could mean nothing. A competitive nature was more than important; it was essential.

★ ★ ★ ★ ★ ★ ★ ★ ★ ★ ★ ★ ★

Bill adjusted his ball cap and smiled. "Your bay colt's not scared. He's not intimidated. He gives it right back to that little tough guy. But then, once inside the barn, your big bay is as nice as can be. Learns fast too."

Gretchen chuckled as Bill told more stories of how her bay colt and Last Best Place played chase and horse-wrestled until they both lay down in exhaustion. Such hard play was making them both strong and tough.

"But how has he taken to the halter?" Roy asked. If an athlete wasn't easy to train, he'd be a benchwarmer for life. And with a horse, it could make the difference between the one who won races and the one who threw away all his energy *cutting up* at the races.

"Oh, well," Bill said, "your colt hasn't faltered with a halter. Not even once."

Gretchen pulled out her camera and snapped pictures of her new colt. She then went to see the others Bill had foaled for her from other mares. But as she walked, she turned to look back at the big bay colt, who was now running across the pasture with Last Best Place, neck and neck, while their mothers ate grass. The mares knew the two babies might play rough and run like wild, crazy things, but in a minute both babies would flop down nearby to sleep away the afternoon.

Last Best Place galloped as if his legs were windmills harnessing air. He was pushing La Ville's colt to greater

★ ★ ★ ★ ★ ★ ★ ★ ★ ★ ★ ★ ★

and greater speed. They were following the fence in longer and longer distances, around and around the pasture. La Ville's colt ran as though any minute he'd catch a breeze and rise into the air to soar past Last Best Place in a mocking tease, saying, *Run, run as fast as you can. You can't catch me. You call that* speed? *Look again, little guy. I'm about to fly!*

And the small red colt was using his thundering legs to tease back. *Oh yeah, oh yeah. You brag, but you'll lag. I'll catch you before you can say "hot bran mash" and "cold oat soup." You're the one who's going to end up—burned toast!*

After the Jacksons drove off, Bill Sanborn went out to the big pasture and hooked a lead rope to La Ville's colt's halter. It was time for a bath. But after a moment of obediently following Bill, the colt suddenly stopped. He took a step back.

"Ho there, kiddo," Bill remarked. "Don't make a liar out of me. I said you'd never faltered on a halter."

Barbaro looked at Bill with wide eyes. His head was up like a giraffe's, and he wore a mischievous look. He wouldn't budge. Bending his neck, he tried to look back at Last Best Place. He didn't want to leave his friend, even for the short while it would take to have a bath.

The red colt stood by his mother, eating as though he didn't care a thing about the bay colt who was his best playmate.

★ ★ ★ ★ ★ ★ ★ ★ ★ ★ ★ ★ ★ ★

Bill looped the lead rope around Barbaro's rear, capturing the colt in a circle that could push and pull at the same time. He pulled the rope gently but firmly. "Come on now. You know the rules. You're just trying to copy your tough-guy friend and give me trouble."

Barbaro moved one step forward. Then he took a few more steps closer to the barn. It was as if he then remembered who he was and that every person he'd ever known had been his friend. Obediently he walked into the barn.

Quietly Barbaro stood while Bill turned on the hose, took out the soap, and bathed him until he was shining as bright as polished wood in a great cathedral. And like the mysteries that a great church watches over, locked safely away inside Barbaro, waiting patiently, was the secret of what this big colt would be one day.

★ ★ ★ ★ ★ ★ ★ ★ ★ ★ ★ ★ ★ ★

★ CHAPTER 5 ★

Parting Is More Than Sweet Sorrow

EVERY MONTH BILL SANBORN READ the changes in the planets and the stars. He followed them and weaned his foals according to what a calendar of these signs told him. Like a lot of horsemen, he believed in separating foals from their mothers on a special day. And he chose this time the same way a farmer would look in a farmer's almanac to choose the best time for a plant to grow. So when Barbaro was five months old, Bill clipped a rope onto the colt's halter and led him to a pasture where Last Best Place was already running, calling for his mother.

She was in another pasture, far away. She was calling too. La Ville Rouge was with her. Both mares and foals sounded frightened and unsure.

★　★　★　★　★　★　★　★　★　★　★

*I'm here. Where are you? Are you there? Where is there? I'm
here. I'm okay. Are you? Answer me! Answer me!*

The horse calls between dam and foal went back
and forth, back and forth. At least Barbaro had his best
friend, Last Best Place, to go through this difficult time
with him. They had to be weaned. They no longer needed
their mothers' milk. They ate grass now, and grain. And
their mothers were already pregnant with other foals to
be born in the spring.

Although Barbaro came into the world on April
29, like all Thoroughbreds he claimed the first day of
January as his birthday. That way, all young horses can
begin racing at the same time. And since it is desirable
that foals be born when the weather is good, mares
become pregnant eleven months before each spring. It
was time now for Barbaro to move on, to give up his life
with his mother. He was nearly half a year old. When he
was one year old, he would be called a yearling and be
ready to train as the athlete he would become.

Barbaro and Last Best Place continued to call
frantically to their mothers. The mares whinnied; the
colts answered. They were too troubled to eat. But then
after a while the mares put their heads down into the
lush grass. They nibbled a little.

Barbaro and Last Best Place began pulling at the
rich green too. Slowly and for a longer time, they began

★　★　★　★　★　★　★　★　★　★　★　★　★　★

to forget they were no longer with their mothers. The mares forgot they no longer had their babies at their sides. Each shared the paddock with another horse, so none was alone. And since horses are vegetarians, their instincts were telling them to eat, eat, graze as many hours as they could. One never knew when bad weather or danger was coming, and it took a lot of grass to fill up their big horse bodies.

Eating was the strongest instinct they had.

In a few hours Barbaro and Last Best Place began to play together, just as they had when their mothers had been with them.

They were on their own now, out in the world, soon to be trained to do what they had been born to do. Running was in them the same way a plant knows what color to bloom.

Every three to four days another foal and mother were separated, and the foal herd grew. Now there was a group of seven or eight to run with. And always Barbaro or Last Best Place would be in the lead. Barbaro and Last Best Place bit each other and kicked and ran and bucked, swapping off as leaders of their tiny herd.

Throughout that year, whenever Gretchen and Roy Jackson came to look at their big bay colt, Roy would ask, "Decided on a name yet?"

And Gretchen would answer, "No. And I don't want

★ ★ ★ ★ ★ ★ ★ ★ ★ ★ ★ ★ ★

to rush. This one deserves a special name. And when I hear the right name, I'll know it." She watched the bay colt scampering around like popcorn in a popper. He was also now growing like a stalk of corn, tall and slim. A kind but mischievous look sparkled in his eyes, especially when he was turned out with Last Best Place.

In September, Barbaro began following a schedule that would slowly make him ready to take his place on a racetrack. Every few days he was bathed and his whiskers were clipped. His mane was pulled so it was thin enough to lie to one side yet short enough to stay out of his way. He was tied up to a ring in his stall for short periods while he was groomed. He learned patience and obedience this way.

Every morning he was turned out, and each night he was brought into his stall. He wore a halter whenever he was in the pasture, and Bill unbuckled it every night so it could not accidentally get caught on anything in Barbaro's stall. That could be dangerous. All horses have a natural fear of being trapped; all are a bit claustrophobic. Being prey animals, they panic if they are not free to run. And overcoming that fear is what they learn from those who take care of them.

Always, Bill handled Barbaro and talked to him as though he were a little kid learning his ABCs. Barbaro was agreeable and quick to learn his lessons, but his deep intelligence and patience did not show itself completely until the day Bill brought the colt into the barn and saw the bump on the inside of his front leg.

"Oh my goodness, kiddo," he exclaimed, patting the colt. "Looks like you and Last Best Place got too rough. Most likely you've hit yourself racing around. Okay, big guy, we'll have to attend to this."

The small lump on the inside of Barbaro's leg, called a "splint," was hot to the touch. A splint is not really a serious injury, but it needs to be attended to. Barbaro had probably banged that splint bone with one of his other legs. It happens often that a foal strikes himself while playing hard. The splint bone, next to the big bone in the leg, was swelling from a calcium deposit forming there. This was nature's way of sort of gluing the splint bone to the big bone, so the leg would grow strong.

Bill led Barbaro into the barn and put him in a stall with a cutout in the door. Right away Barbaro stuck his head through that dip in the stall door. And for the next two weeks, he watched everything that went on all day in the big barn.

Maybe Barbaro was thinking human beings were fun to watch. Maybe he was thinking he could have taught them a thing or two. At the least, he probably thought he could teach them how to make dinner come faster.

Near the end of the second week, Bill studied the

★ ★ ★ ★ ★ ★ ★ ★ ★ ★ ★ ★

big bay colt who so patiently accepted staying in his stall so he could heal. The colt had learned to be satisfied just by watching.

"You're a patient one, aren't you, big guy? You'll be back tussling with your friend in a day or two."

Fretting and fighting got him nowhere; Barbaro was smart enough to figure that out. Besides, he'd always enjoyed human company.

Soon he was again running and playing with Last Best Place. In the spring, after their birthdays, they were one-year-old colts—tall and healthy, aware of their strength. They were ready to be sent away as yearlings for training.

In her home in Pennsylvania, Gretchen Jackson fretted. Where, oh where, would she find the name for the big bay colt? She looked for it to appear in a book she was reading. She listened for the lyrics in a song to catch her attention and become a name. But nothing spoke to her. Nothing seemed to fit the big bay colt.

On September 17, 2004, Bill led the yearling, yet to be named Barbaro, into a big van to take his place beside ten other horses. All were on their way to training farms. Bill took off the colt's halter to turn him loose in a box stall filled with deep straw. Hay hung in a net, and a water bucket was filled to the rim.

Bill said good-bye to La Ville Rouge's colt for the

★ ★ ★ ★ ★ ★ ★ ★ ★ ★ ★ ★ ★ ★

last time and walked back to the barn. The van's motor started with a loud chugging, like a cough. Then it settled into a deep hum. The van eased off down the driveway.

Last Best Place stood in the paddock eating, unaware that his friend was leaving. He, too, would leave soon. He, too, would soon start his career as the racehorse he was bred to be.

La Ville Rouge grazed contentedly in a pasture, heavy in foal with a brother to the big bay colt, who had yet to wear his own name. Parting was more than sweet sorrow. It was the beginning of a promise they were all keeping.

A speed song was building in the big bay colt, humming deep in his bones, blood, and heart. He had only to hear it now. He had only to let the rhythm of the song catch his feet.

He set off on his journey to discover how well he could hear the music.

★ ★ ★ ★ ★ ★ ★ ★ ★ ★ ★ ★ ★ ★

CHAPTER 6

What a Bummer!

ALL THROUGH THE NIGHT THE VAN rumbled through the countryside, ticking away the miles. It moved through three states, stopping only to give the horses water. Down through Kentucky, across Tennessee, over to Georgia, and straight into Florida. It pulled into an inspection station, and the driver got out.

He opened a book to show the papers for each of the ten horses on board. How could any of them be carrying a disease to spread to a horse in Florida? They'd been given shots galore! But proof had to be shown, for protecting each horse from a contagious disease was more than a matter of kindness. It was extremely important.

Inside, Barbaro was eating hay in his box stall, being good. But like any yearling, he was itching to buck and roll, jump and

★　★　★　★　★　★　★　★　★　★　★

play. Miles, though, were still left to go. Outside, the September sky was as dark as inside the toe of a sock. Dawn was hours away.

Finally the big van turned down a curving driveway. The horses inside did not know they had reached their destination.

The van driver pulled up under giant oak trees. Rays of sun came through their branches. Fog hung in the air like the sleeve on a ghost's shirt.

"Van's here," someone called, and the message spread. One worker to another called, "Van's here." "It's here." "Here."

"*Aquí, aquí,*" Spanish words of "Here, here," floated from some workers to others. And cell phones spread the word.

Each horse was carefully led down the ramp of the van. Barbaro put his head up to sniff the air. There was the smell of damp earth—yep, and there was also the smell of manure. Lots of it. And somewhere nearby, a skunk had passed through in the night. This place was certainly not like Kentucky. The Florida air felt cool at dawn, but balmy—somewhat like a coating from a soft steam bath.

The oak trees were at least a hundred years old. Their trunks were as wide as three fat men hugging in a circle. The trees' branches spread like umbrellas overhead.

★ ★ ★ ★ ★ ★ ★ ★ ★ ★ ★ ★ ★ ★

Inside the barn the ten yearlings clopped, their baby-size hooves stepping on the concrete floor. They came in like a train, and the owners of the farm, John and Jill Stephens, came to watch. They were opening file folders, ready to write.

Each horse was lined up to have its photo taken. The picture would be stapled into a file to help identify each.

Every horse's markings were noted—a blaze, a star, a snip on the nose, white on a leg, a scar here or there. After all, over the eight months they would spend at this training farm, they would change. Some would grow two or three inches or more. And there were so many horses coming in almost every day. Through the year, eighty or more would arrive.

Barbaro stood quietly in the aisle of the barn while his handler stepped back to be out of the way of the camera lens. And then *click*, the film caught him, just as he took a step. *Click* again as he stood still. The camera saved his image for all time, looking like the yearling he was—lanky, awkward, his shoulder as long as a plank of wood. Power was there to be made and molded.

But in this picture he was only seventeen months old. With one year in a horse's life equaling about three of a human's life, Barbaro was like a kid arriving for his first day in preschool. And his picture showed it. He was all legs and scruffy mane. His head looked too big for

★ ★ ★ ★ ★ ★ ★ ★ ★ ★ ★ ★ ★ ★

his body. His tail was no longer than a fireplace broom.

No one was thinking he was anything special at all.

A groom rolled the protective wraps off his legs. And as soon as the colt's front legs were exposed, a sound went up that traveled through the barn. "*Aquí.* Here, this one. Come look at this one. *Aquí. Aquí.* Two splints here. Don't turn this horse out."

From somewhere too came the universal sound of concern. "Uh-oh!"

Jill Stephens bent down to run her fingers over the hard knots on the insides of Barbaro's front legs. Yes, there were splints here. Not just one now, but two. Maybe he had smacked himself in the van or somewhere else. In any case, one large knot was now on each of his front legs. And since serious training was about to start, the splints certainly needed to be attended to.

Jill called the vet.

The other yearlings were being hand-walked and turned into a round pen outside to stretch their legs. But Barbaro was led into a stall and the door was closed.

What a bummer. He was going to have to be still again—for days, maybe weeks. Yep, definitely, this was a bummer.

He whinnied, calling to the other horses nearby, as his way of saying, *I'm here. Where are you? And by the way, where is* here?

On his stall door, a nameplate was hung. "La Ville Rouge" and "Dynaformer" were written in the spaces beside the words "dam" and "sire." He was known only as the son of his parents. For all the months he would be in this horse kindergarten he would wear the name of his father, "the Dynaformer colt."

In another few minutes the bay colt settled down as he always did. He sniffed the stall shavings and looked for food. More or less his attitude had always been, *Whatever, whatever.* His stall here felt pretty much like any other.

From somewhere came the smell of alfalfa hay wafting up over the stall door and into his nose. To a horse, alfalfa is the equivalent of a juicy hamburger with piping hot fries and a frothy milk shake. Or better yet, a piece of chocolate cake.

As for those splints—only the humans were concerned. They were the ones sending for the vet, then taking the colt's temperature to make sure he hadn't picked up a cold on his trip.

The colt himself cared only about the flake of hay sitting outside his stall. *When in the world would it ever be dinnertime?* How could he get someone to pick up that hay and throw it in to him? He nickered as a man passed.

But the man did not turn to look at the new horse.

★ ★ ★ ★ ★ ★ ★ ★ ★ ★ ★ ★ ★

He did not stop to throw the hay into the stall.

Wow, what a bummer! More than anything, the big bay colt loved to eat. And more than anything, he wanted to figure out how to get dinner served early.

★ ★ ★ ★ ★ ★ ★ ★ ★ ★ ★ ★ ★ ★ ★

CHAPTER 7

A Tooth for a Tooth

THE YEARLING DUTIFULLY CAME out of his stall, led by a groom. The vet gave him a shot to sedate him, then fired the splints on his front legs. "Fired" sounds harsh, but it means only that great heat was applied to the top of the hardened lumps. The heat signaled his body to send new blood cells to the injured site.

New bone growth would now weld the injured splint bone to the cannon bone, the largest bone in a horse's leg. It would heal and be strong, very strong.

"He'll be fit as a fiddle, in time," the vet said. "Just give him rest."

Jill Stephens stood close, making notes to put in Barbaro's file. "And I paint them with the medicine you gave me, every day?"

★ ★ ★ ★ ★ ★ ★ ★ ★ ★ ★

"Yes. His front legs won't be a thing of beauty. He'll be left with a blemish. But a blemish is a blemish. It's nothing to affect his performance in any way. He'll be as sound as a metal wash pot, once these heal."

"And hand-walking?"

"In a few weeks you can start that. Then walk him twice a day. In six to eight weeks he'll be ready to put into training."

Jill Stephens led Barbaro back into his stall. "You have to stay here and be quiet," she said, picking up a brush. She brushed the yearling for a long while, knowing this was something he had experienced in other places. It would make him feel relaxed and at home.

Jill's voice, a few notes above a middle C on a piano, was reassuring. It also had a way of going up and down, lilting on a sentence, adding sweetness. Medium tall and willowlike, she was as thin as a pine tree.

She could easily reach the back of the young horse. He was tall for a yearling, but no taller than fifteen hands and three inches. He would grow an enormous amount after his second birthday, but no one knew that now. They saw him only as the awkward yearling he was.

In the way that horses are measured, with four inches to each hand, fifteen hands and three inches meant Barbaro was four times fifteen plus three. That measured out at five feet, three inches at the top of his back, called

★ ★ ★ ★ ★ ★ ★ ★ ★ ★ ★ ★ ★ ★

the withers, which is the bony rise where a horse's mane ends. Jill was five feet, five inches herself, so she could easily move the brush over every part of him, up his neck to his head. And Barbaro leaned into the brush with pleasure, asking for more.

Jill's blond hair was pulled into a ponytail. Her skin was suntanned to the shade of a Christmas cookie. Cinnamon-colored freckles dotted her face. She smiled often, speaking softly to the yearling colt. "You'll be fine here. You just have to be still and wait awhile. Then we'll have some fun."

She always talked to horses as if they understood every word she said. It was the sound of her voice and her mood they understood. In the tone of her voice they read what she meant—praise and affection or displeasure and disapproval.

To Jill, loving horses was like breathing. For four generations her family had worked at a racetrack It was her grandfather who'd taught her to watch the horse's eyes to see changes in its mood, to study the horse's ears to receive messages about what it might do. She knew to move quietly and carefully. The whole while, she was reading the horse's body language as skillfully as she would read a page in a book.

She walked out of the stall and closed the door. Barbaro followed her, sniffing through the door. Being stalled and kept inside was hard, but he had done it

★ ★ ★ ★ ★ ★ ★ ★ ★ ★ ★ ★ ★

before. He had just not been confined for this long the last time.

"When your splints have healed, we'll move you over to my school," Jill said. The big bay colt looked at her with his dark brown eyes. He seemed to accept what she said even if he did not understand it.

As the vet left, John Stephens came to the stall to inquire about the Dynaformer yearling.

"Weeks and weeks," Jill said, filling him in on the treatment.

John opened the stall door and walked in. He looked closely at the Dynaformer colt. Having worked with horses for more than thirty years, John Stephens had a deep understanding about how to train them. He patted the colt. His hand was firm and soothing. In John's office he kept a roping saddle he had won at a rodeo. He wore jeans, a T-shirt, a ball cap, and boots.

Here was someone knowledgeable about everything a yearling would face in his first school. Here was someone who knew how to give a young horse skills to live out his job as a racehorse.

John's blue eyes, curious and kind, studied the colt. Once the yearling finished Jill's school, John would be the one to take over his training. "Patience. Patience. We can never have enough of it," he said, and stepped back.

Something unusual about the horse caught his

attention. In the colt's eyes he read an intelligence. But there was also another quality, difficult to name. He had seen it in a variety of animals, especially those living in the wild, where they might be hunted or face great danger. Ah, yes, this horse had *savvy*. That was the word he would use. "Savvy"—meaning this colt possessed common sense. This was a horse not likely to do anything foolish. He was sensible and, even now, gentlemanly.

"I'll see you one day," John said confidently, patting the colt. Then he walked out to the racetrack, where he was supervising young horses' workouts.

The next day the horse dentist came. Oh, this training barn was never at a loss for activity!

The dentist sedated Barbaro and pulled his wolf teeth, the two long fanglike teeth that had come in after his milk teeth. Like a human child, a young horse's first teeth are replaced by adult teeth. And Barbaro would now be getting new teeth each year until he was five. They would even grow continuously over his lifetime. The way they changed would tell his age.

Since horses don't eat meat, they don't need sharp teeth. Sure, sharp teeth might have been useful to a young stallion in a fight in the wild. But these wolf teeth would serve no purpose for Barbaro, and a wide space was needed between his front teeth and molars in order for a bit to fit comfortably.

★ ★ ★ ★ ★ ★ ★ ★ ★ ★ ★ ★ ★ ★

Vets. Dentists. Splints to be healed. Temperature to be taken. Was there no end to this?

Barbaro looked through the mesh in the stall door and watched people walk by.

Day after day he waited and watched. He heard Spanish words, and English. He saw people move quietly and purposefully. He learned to draw on the quietness within the center of himself. He learned to wait and be still, and then to wait some more.

Inside him it was as if his body had a clock memorizing the days. At daylight there was feed. At lunchtime there was more. Overhead a mist of fly spray, as cool as ice water, came out of a nozzle and spread over the stall. Several times his water buckets were scrubbed and refilled. After all, a horse drinks at least twelve gallons in a day.

Sometimes a heat lamp would come on. The pupils in his eyes would read the light as a long day. And it would signal his coat to not grow as thick and shaggy as if he were outside and needing a heavy winter coat. He was staying slick and shiny.

At three o'clock the last few handfuls of sweet feed were poured into his feed bin. Oh, it was such a pitiful, disappointing amount. The amount of grain he got had been cut down because he was getting about as much exercise as a fat, no-good mouse hiding in the tack room.

★　★　★　★　★　★　★　★　★　★　★　★　★

At eight o'clock the Mexican man named Vicente and his wife, Elvia, with the long black flowing hair, came and walked slowly through the barn. They looked into each stall, checking on each horse. And then the barn lights would go off.

The colt stayed quiet and accepted each day as it came.

Little did anyone know then, every lesson the bay yearling was learning here would help him—two years later—to hold on to his life.

★ ★ ★ ★ ★ ★ ★ ★ ★ ★ ★ ★ ★ ★

CHAPTER 8

Row, Row, Row Your Boat

IN THE MIDDLE OF OCTOBER, JILL took the Dynaformer colt out of his stall and led him to her shed-row barn. An aisle ran all the way around the stalls, like a porch. Beside the barn two palm trees grew with leaves like a fan of spikes. As Jill and the colt passed them, Barbaro reached to eat one. "Oh, no you don't." Jill pulled him away.

"Lesson one," Jill said, leading Barbaro into a stall and brushing him so he would feel at home there, too. She expected him to be wild after being cooped up for so long. She stood on guard, ready to move aside quickly if he kicked out or stomped around. And as always she wore a padded vest, gloves, and a jockey's helmet.

★　★　★　★　★　★　★　★　★　★

Soon Barbaro was licking his lips and chewing, a sign Jill could read. It was his way of saying he was ready to follow her lead. He was relaxed now and not worried. Jill smiled. She knew he was always a sucker for a soft brush on his neck and down his chest. Under her hand she could feel his body sigh and relax.

Here at this farm, Jill and John Stephens wanted to make each yearling ready to be a racehorse—not just physically but mentally, too. The horses should *like* their jobs and have the skills to survive years living at a racetrack, running for a living. "Very few are special," John often said, "but they all have the drive to compete. And here, they are all on the same starting line."

John also knew a horse wouldn't survive if it were trained by concentrating on speed only. He designed each yearling's schooling to its own needs. He worried as much about a horse's mind as its body. A horse should run for fun. And he and Jill wanted to help each yearling become the best athlete possible.

Fear was the challenge. After all, fear was laced through Barbaro's brain, just as fear lived in any horse's mind—going back thousands of years to when a horse was no bigger than a fox. More than fifty million years ago, in the age after the dinosaurs called the Eocene, the first horses, called eohippus, meaning "dawn horse," had

★   ★   ★   ★   ★   ★   ★   ★   ★   ★   ★   ★   ★

toes on each foot. Eventually, over thousands of years, the toes became one hoof, and the animal grew tall.

About ten thousand years ago, horses disappeared from America altogether. Perhaps they became extinct because of hunting and human settlement. European settlers brought horses back to America, and Indian tribes built their culture around them, as did other groups of people, until the automobile arrived.

Now on this October day in Florida, remnants of this history ran like threads in a long rope, reaching deep into Barbaro's brain. Jill watched him for signs of fear. More like cats than dogs, horses can leap faster than a frog's tongue can catch a fly. Their relationship with people is built entirely on memory, and Jill wanted to make sure everything that happened to Barbaro today would be remembered as kind and good.

In only a few minutes she had him wearing a bridle, with a snaffle bit lying in his mouth. She wanted to give him a lot to feel and get used to. She wanted to see how he would react. He stood still, as though saying, *Whatever, Whatever. Just don't work me past lunch.*

Jill put a martingale—like a leather collar—over his chest and set a light saddle on his back. She then walked him around in his stall. Every few feet she stopped and held her gloved hand up like a crossing guard at a bus stop and said, "Ho." Over and over, Barbaro heard "Ho,"

"Ho," "Ho,"—which was a shortened form of "Whoa." That was it. Lesson over.

The memory track in Barbaro's head took the sound of "Ho" and held it, as quickly as he'd learned the squeak of the feed cart coming down the barn aisle.

These lessons were a piece of cake for him.

In seven days Barbaro knew three sounds and four English words. He was trotting around a sixty-foot circle on a long line called a "lunge," with Jill calling out, "Jog," "Walk," "Gallop," and "Ho." She made a smooching sound, which meant to gallop, and a clucking sound, which meant to go faster. *Oh, yeah*, Barbaro seemed to say. *Whatever, whatever.*

She popped the lunge whip. It was long with a loose piece at the end, which made a sound like a firecracker. But the sound didn't mean Jill wanted Barbaro to lunge and leap forward like a wild, crazy thing. Instead, Barbaro learned that Jill used the lunge whip like an extension of her arm.

This whip was not a hungry animal chasing him, and it was not ever going to abuse him. But he regarded it and its sound with respect. It kept him awake and thinking. It was like a person gesturing with hands while talking. *Pop, pop, pop.* And then, "Uh-uh! Now cut it out," Jill would call when he bucked and acted like a kid set free at recess after being cooped up in a classroom. "You're not very good at listening today. I'm not impressed. Let's try again."

But what did she expect? There was a whole paddock of fillies nearby.

A mystery lurked at the woods. Exercise riders jogged horses around giant oaks. Some went into the woods and disappeared down a path there. Barbaro put his head up and sniffed, watching. Every day horses with people perched on their backs went to the woods and disappeared.

October, November. The days moved to a rhythm of their own. He was now turned out into a paddock for half the day to run and buck, just like any yearling. And often one of the farmworkers would say, "Look at him cut the fool!"

Every morning sunlight threaded through the tree canopy in yellow-white streaks. Doves cooed. Yearlings nickered. The soft clicking of Spanish words floated back and forth between workers like a song. There was a calm, lazy sweetness to the days. The trees and grass seemed to sing the song that the earth always knows. There was a soothing cadence here.

The days were like a mountain stream, meandering, curving, and weaving at a slow pace. It was as if the hours were singing, *Row, row, row your boat, gently down the stream. Merrily, merrily, merrily, merrily, life is but a dream.*

★ ★ ★ ★ ★ ★ ★ ★ ★ ★ ★ ★ ★ ★ ★

What the bay yearling was dreaming, no one knew. Not even his own ears could yet hear the pulsing, growing rhythm that, one day, would explode through his hooves.

★ ★ ★ ★ ★ ★ ★ ★ ★ ★ ★ ★ ★ ★ ★

★ CHAPTER 9 ★

Rhythm and Shoes

THE PATH THROUGH THE WOODS continued to be a haunting mystery. On some days Barbaro got close to finding out where it led. Jill hooked long reins called "long lines" on to the bay colt's bridle and drove him, as though he were pulling a cart, all over the farm. But it was only her walking behind him. "That's right. Go ahead. I'm with you. Don't worry. Go," she'd say.

If they started on the path through the woods, she always made him turn around before they reached the end.

Jill drove him between trees and past paddocks and fields. She made him pass through scary places and walk past rocks that looked like crouching monsters. Always she spoke reassuringly to him, "It's all right. Go on. I'm behind you."

★ ★ ★ ★ ★ ★ ★ ★ ★ ★ ★

If he became unsure of himself, she stopped and led him through the place that was scaring him. She never let him lose his confidence. And she never taught him a new thing until she sensed he was ready for it.

She showed him how to turn in a loop whenever she said, "Change." She marveled at how quickly the colt learned new things. They walked miles and miles together like this. And all the while, Barbaro was building a word bank of English and Spanish, just like a kid learning to read. He could also now understand how these humans talked with *their* bodies. The way they moved said everything.

Jill was learning too that if she didn't keep the Dynaformer colt busy, he was likely to get into trouble and lose his focus. It was clear he loved to learn. And she worked hard to keep him busy.

The long reins were teaching the colt where his engine was. After all, there was a person walking behind him, carrying the whip that was an extension of her arm. And she was always signaling, *Go on, go on. It's all right. Go on.* The bay colt learned she would not ask him to do something unless she thought it was safe. He put his trust in her, and she never let him down.

Since all horses carry more than half their weight on their front feet, the bay colt didn't really understand what his back legs were for. Well, yes, they were handy

★ ★ ★ ★ ★ ★ ★ ★ ★ ★ ★ ★ ★ ★ ★

at keeping him upright when he was asleep, like a bike's kickstand. In fact, there were ligaments that would lock so he could stand up and sleep. That way he was always ready to run if danger came. But now Jill was teaching him to engage his back legs and muscles for another reason. He was learning to be an athlete. And all the while, he didn't have the extra problem of carrying a rider on his back while he was learning this.

The colt was finding out his body wanted to do more than eat.

When the day came to ride him for the first time, Jill first lay across his back in the stall. Then slowly, over several days, when the look in his eyes told her he was ready, she sat up in the saddle and rode him in the stall in circles. Just like with everything else she had thrown at him, he learned this, to carry her, like a gentleman. And when she taught him that carrying a rider was no more trouble than asking someone to dance, she passed him on to one of the exercise riders.

Soon Barbaro was walking out into the field with a rider on his back, just like all the older yearlings. Then he was trotting, learning to balance while the rider moved in partnership with the motion.

One day his rider aimed him to the path through the woods. It was cool and dark there. The live oak trees kept their leaves, even in winter.

★ ★ ★ ★ ★ ★ ★ ★ ★ ★ ★ ★ ★ ★

His rider urged him on. The path ended, and Barbaro emerged from the woods and walked into a wide opening.

Here was a great O. It was not quite a circle. It was more an oval, covered in fog as if it were sitting on a cloud. It was a practice racetrack. It was set on forty-two acres and was bordered by white plastic fencing. Its soil was as soft as velvet powder. Horses were galloping and trotting on it. They moved through the fog like dancers. But after only a brief look Barbaro's rider turned him around and walked him back to the shed row.

On a Monday in early December he sensed something new was about to happen. The day before, a farrier had come and put shoes on all his hooves. He was gripping the ground now like a soccer player wearing cleats.

"Maarteeeeen, you're up," Jill called from the shed row. She put a race saddle and bridle on the Dynaformer colt. The morning was barely light. It was cold, and the colt's rump hair stood up, trapping the air under his hair to keep him warm.

"Take him to John," Jill called to the man walking up. "He'll tell you what to do."

The small Mexican man named Martin, but pronounced "Marteen," put his hand on the saddle and leapt up. He landed lightly on the colt's back. He reached down and put his feet in the stirrups. He wore a padded

★ ★ ★ ★ ★ ★ ★ ★ ★ ★ ★ ★ ★

[Top] A groom shows off six-week-old Barbaro. (PHOTO: GRETCHEN AND ROY JACKSON)

[Bottom] Barbaro's best friend, Last Best Place, as a yearling.
(PHOTO: GRETCHEN AND ROY JACKSON)

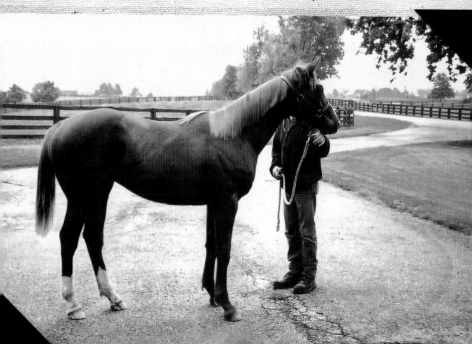

(PHOTO: JEFFREY SNYDER)

[Top left] Barbaro with Peter Brette in an early morning workout at Fair Hill.

[Bottom left] Owner Gretchen Jackson with Barbaro at Churchill Downs during Kentucky Derby week.

(PHOTO: BARBARA LIVINGSTON)

And the winner is. . . . Barbaro's breathtaking Kentucky Derby run.

(PHOTOS: ULI SEIT)

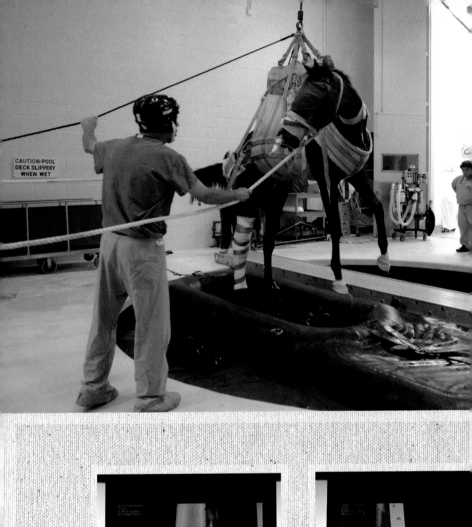

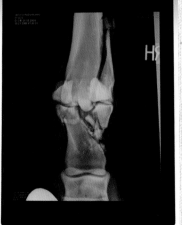

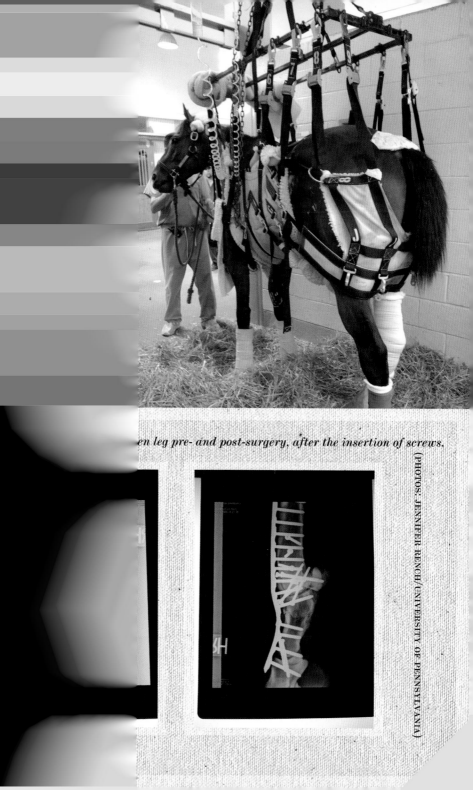

en leg pre- and post-surgery, after the insertion of screws.

[Upper left] Edgar Prado, Barbaro's jockey, visits Barbaro for the first time after the accident.

[Upper right] Cards from well-wishers adorn Barbaro's stall.

[lower left]
...chael Matz,
...rbaro's trainer,
...its him almost
...ry day.

[lower right]
...at a champion
...oys most—
...evening grain.

PHOTOS:
...INA LOUISE PIERCE/
...VERSITY OF
...NSYLVANIA)

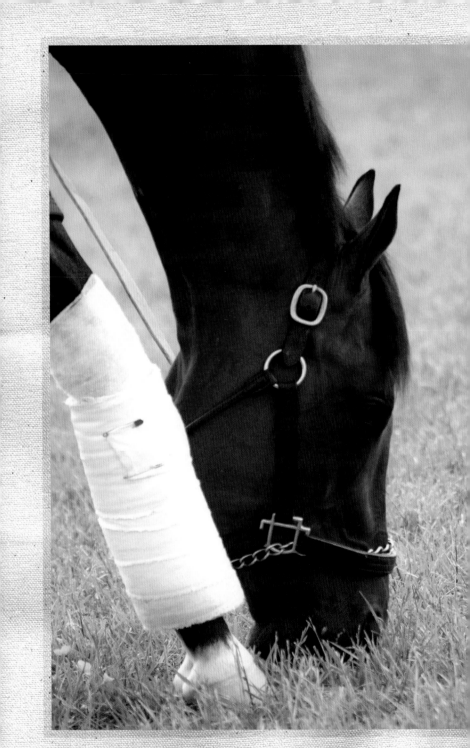

Nothing beats grazing in the grass. (PHOTO: TERESA FERRIS)

vest and a kerchief under a race helmet. His boots were scuffed and worn.

Unsure of his English, he was shy and quiet. He patted the colt and pulled the right rein.

Barbaro turned and headed for the woods.

Where this path led was no longer a secret. The colt now knew its destination, but the purpose of the great O was still clouded in mystery.

This day, Martin walked the Dynaformer colt through the woods and didn't turn back. He walked him through a gate, right onto the great O!

He let the colt move slowly on the track for a while. Then Martin clucked and said, "Jog." Barbaro stepped out into his two-beat rhythm, holding his nose up, sniffing the air. He snorted and weaved. He zigzagged, wanting to put his head down and sniff every manure pile they came across. But Martin kept him trotting, letting the colt curiously look over the track, exploring it.

Martin felt the colt signaling his uncertainty. It was almost as though the big bay yearling was scared of the track. It was clear the Dynaformer colt didn't know what all this was about. He didn't understand where he was going.

It seemed to make no sense. *Why have a path with no end?* This was just a circle, around and around, a mile

★ ★ ★ ★ ★ ★ ★ ★ ★ ★ ★ ★ ★

of soft soil. And there was no way out but through the gate.

The colt lifted his knees higher than usual. It was as if he did not like the feel of the dirt on his new shoes.

John was standing at the rail, and when Barbaro and Martin passed by, John called, "Try a slow gallop." The mist was lifting. It no longer looked so much as if the horses were moving through a cloud.

Martin urged the yearling on. Barbaro broke into the waltz rhythm of a gallop. Easy and light, with legs like a fish's fins sweeping through water, the colt covered the soil as though he were floating. His high-knee movement seemed unusual to Martin and John. But his stride was efficient. He used his legs with no wasted motion.

Martin sat forward and whispered to the colt in part English and part Spanish, "You're doing fine, little *caballo. Tranquilo, amigo mio,* be calm, my little friend."

As Barbaro and Martin again passed John, John called out, "Get him up into the bit. Let him do it on his own, but don't let him go too fast."

Martin gripped the reins with firmness, yet with an elastic feel. The colt stretched his mouth into the support of Martin's hands on the bit and felt his neck balance his long body. His feet moved farther up under him. It was as if he were saying a long, loud *AHHHH.*

For the first time the colt felt the power of the

engine that nature had given him. His back legs and strong hips were like pistons and axles—similar to the steel-hard structure of a machine that could scamper up mountains, even pull a tractor out of mud. His lungs drew deep breaths. *So. This is what* this *is all about.*

The Dynaformer colt stretched his whole body low to the track.

If a horse can feel glee, it was glee, indeed, that Barbaro was feeling. It moved all through him, from his ears to his hooves. His body began soaring in delight.

And if he could have said what he was thinking, no doubt it was only a few words of simple truth: *This is who I am. This is what—all along—my blood has been whispering to me.*

Yes, this was the rhythm he was meant to dance to. This was the Dynaformer colt who would soon wear the name of Barbaro. This was where he would write his name in the soil as a legend.

★ ★ ★ ★ ★ ★ ★ ★ ★ ★ ★ ★

★ **CHAPTER 10** ★

Lickety-Split, Nobody Here Sits

FOUR MONTHS LATER, AT THE END of April, one day before the colt's second birthday, a van pulled up next to the barn. A groom led Barbaro up into it.

Over the past month his yearling training had been finished. He'd learned from John how to walk into a starting gate. He knew to be quiet there and not be afraid. He had galloped miles slowly. Parts of other miles he had galloped rather fast. He was fit. And his muscles were hard. Galloping had helped him grow bone. He had become taller. He was now well over sixteen hands tall.

The van pulled off in the afternoon and turned left, heading east. All night the van traveled to another farm Barbaro

★ ★ ★ ★ ★ ★ ★ ★ ★ ★

had never seen. Still carrying only his father's name, the Dynaformer colt nudged his hay bag with his nose. *Whatever. Whatever.* He locked his legs in his sleeping pose and dozed through the night.

In the morning he would figure out where he was.

That afternoon John and Jill went into the office and wrote the last words they would put into the Dynaformer colt's file. *Working a good 1/4 mile and galloping out 3/8ths. Has galloped away from the gates. No problems to speak of. He is a lovely ride. You're going to be happy with him.*

In Pennsylvania, on the farm where she and Roy lived, Gretchen Jackson later read these words as she stood in the hallway of her house. A picture hanging on the wall there was catching her attention in a new way. She was eager to give a name to her big bay colt now, and suddenly she had found the perfect name to fit him.

She was gazing at the picture. It had been handed down in Roy's family and was very old. It was a print called a lithograph, which meant the surface around the subjects had been cut away, then pressed down into ink. So the outlines picked up the darkness and the image stayed light. This gave the picture a playful charm as it showed six foxhounds, big energetic dogs that liked to chase foxes. And their faces were lined up, looking directly at the person who was standing there looking at them. All the dogs had names inked in under their faces. The very first one was named Barbaro. The word in Spanish meant "savage," and also "fantastic." But that was not the reason Gretchen wanted the big bay colt to wear the name. It was that playful confidence in the foxhound's eyes that she had seen in her colt. They were perfect kindred spirits.

Roy and Gretchen Jackson now planned to go down the line of all the foxhounds in the picture, naming their foals after them when they were born.

So it was in the early morning of April 29, on his second birthday, that the bay colt arrived in the big van and walked down the ramp to see where he was. He put his nose up to sniff. The air was crisp. It was about six a.m. The sun was barely up. A fog hung over the ground like a tissue being lifted.

From near a big barn, a hill rose up. At its top, in the mist, a racetrack looked like a waiting room in heaven. Horses with riders galloped on the track and disappeared into the white, foggy air.

People and horses seemed to be everywhere. Horses being ridden, horses being hand-walked, horses being given showers at the back of the barn—they were all so busy! Others were rolling and bucking around in their own makeshift corrals, made out of metal and placed across the green grass like private rooms of clover.

A rhythm seemed to thump under all of it. It was

★ ★ ★ ★ ★ ★ ★ ★ ★ ★ ★ ★ ★ ★

like a drum keeping all the footsteps going in the same direction. Everything here was moving lickety-split. Nobody was sitting down. Nobody was waiting for something to happen. Everyone wore a sense of purpose.

Clearly this wasn't kindergarten anymore. This was more like high school or a jump straight into college.

A small Mexican man led Barbaro into the first stall in the big new barn. The bedding here was deep straw, as soft and thick as expensive carpet. The young horse put his nose down and sniffed. He lifted his legs high, feeling out the new footing.

The man clipped the lead on the colt's halter to a ring on the wall, tying him there to be still. The man spoke softly in Spanish and gently tugged the colt's mane, combing the thick black hair with his fingers. "Eduardo," he said. "I am Eduardo."

He had been assigned to be the groom to the big colt for all the months the horse would live there. Eduardo would become the horse's daily companion, even going with him to every race. But that was months away. Those race days were still a mystery to the young horse; only people understood that plan.

Eduardo reached down into a grooming box and pulled out a brush. Now, for the first time, the young horse's name was spoken. The name was the same in any language.

★　★　★　★　★　★　★　★　★　★　★　★　★

"*Aquí*, Barbaro. You are here now, Barbaro."

With the young colt's dignified presence and intelligent eyes, there would never be the need for a nickname or barn name. He was Barbaro. Simply Barbaro.

After his grooming, during which Eduardo carefully looked him over to see if he'd made the long trip okay, Barbaro stood by the door of his new stall, hoping for breakfast. After all, wasn't it time? He'd ridden in the van all night with no grain, only water and hay. Where was the good stuff? Where was the sweet feed? Where was that wonderful grain stirred with molasses? And the hay like chocolate cake?

The trainer, Michael Matz, came to look at the new arrival. He stepped into the stall, wearing jeans, boots with spurs, a Windbreaker, and a ball cap. His eyes, rimmed with smile lines, studied the colt thoughtfully. "Big, pretty, and impressive," he said, touching the two-year-old colt's big shoulder and appreciating the deep intelligence in the young horse's eyes. The man's voice was calm and gentle, somewhat like a low note on a clarinet.

The training center veterinarian, Dr. Kathy Anderson, came to look at the new horse too. A small woman with short salt-and-pepper hair and a kind face, she rubbed the colt's forehead and admired the promise of his size.

★ ★ ★ ★ ★ ★ ★ ★ ★ ★ ★ ★ ★

"You will like it here," she whispered. "It's a good place to be."

And indeed it was. The days moved like a train with a certain destination in mind. And soon Barbaro was getting fourteen quarts a day of that wonderful sweet feed and as much timothy hay as he wanted. It was made from timothy grass and tasted almost like alfalfa. It was just not quite as rich as alfalfa. And it had big fat stalks that took a long time to chew, which was good. It gave him a way to keep busy for much of the day. Chew. Chew. Chew.

He was turned out into a paddock to play and stretch his legs. Eduardo groomed him for a long time each day too, rubbing the young horse with a rubber mitt that could scratch an itch even in a spot that was hard to reach. Barbaro would lift his front leg and paw the air in pleasure. And sometimes he would almost close his eyes and point his top lip as if to say, *More, more, a little higher, yes, yes.*

Sometimes a strange strong smell caught the attention of Barbaro's nose, and he'd lift his top lip and curl it back to show his teeth and gums, as though he were smiling. But really he was just trying to get a better idea of what he was smelling. It was his flehmen response and had nothing to do with how he felt; it had only to do with something in the air that caught his nose's

★ ★ ★ ★ ★ ★ ★ ★ ★ ★ ★ ★ ★

attention. But the reaction made him look exactly as if he were laughing.

Again, for days Barbaro was watched for signs of a cold or other illness. Dr. Anderson went over him carefully, making sure he was sound in every way. Like human babies, young horses have bendable skeletons. Their bones have spaces left open in certain places, so there will be room to grow. At the age of two, horses' knees close. So it would be all right to work Barbaro harder now, and for him to carry more weight.

At the Stephens' farm in Florida, galloping as a yearling had made Barbaro's leg bones strong and thick. He'd never been asked to carry much weight. Every rider had weighed not much more than one hundred pounds. And it would be almost the same here. Dr. Anderson also carefully watched Barbaro for signs of colic. Since horses can't regurgitate—that is, vomit—they have no way to rid themselves of anything in their stomachs that is making them sick. But over those first days after Barbaro's arrival, it was clear he had made the long trip fine. He was healthy and ready to go to work.

On the last day of that first week, a young man named Peter walked into Barbaro's stall and put a racing saddle on his back. The man spoke softly and patted the colt's neck.

Just like all those who had ridden Barbaro as a

★ ★ ★ ★ ★ ★ ★ ★ ★ ★ ★ ★ ★

yearling, this new rider wore a jockey's helmet and a padded vest. But this was the beginning of a partnership that would have a special place in Barbaro's life.

The young man leapt up onto Barbaro's back with a firmness and skill the young horse had not yet felt. Under the jockey's helmet the man's face was sunburned and playful. His eyes wore a steady gaze that was gentle and kind. His words were crisp and wore the sound of England, which is where he had grown up. He had once been a jockey in Dubai, United Arab Emirates, halfway around the world, and had ridden in many races. He was skilled as a competitive jockey.

But here he was the one who would be Barbaro's exercise rider, taking him out every day and turning him into the special athlete he was destined to become. It was this man, Peter Brette, who would help Barbaro find out what he really was.

With Peter in the saddle, Barbaro moved out of the barn and walked up the hill to the practice racetrack, where other young horses were trying out their legs. Dr. Anderson walked by, stopping to look at the new horse going out for a run. She lingered a moment to admire him. Nice horse, she thought. Balanced, rhythmical, athletic. And there was a certain light in his eyes. He seemed really smart.

It was only later that she would say, "We had no idea where he would take us."

★ ★ ★ ★ ★ ★ ★ ★ ★ ★ ★ ★ ★

★ CHAPTER 11 ★

No More Fiddley-Futzing Around

THE SUMMER DAYS WERE LONG AND hot. Early, before the sun was even up, Peter Brette walked into Barbaro's stall carrying his race saddle and bridle. Peter tacked up the young horse and mounted, riding lightly on Barbaro's back. They walked up to the racetrack on the hill in the mist. The first of daylight was the color of dishwater. Blue barely colored the sky.

"You're a big one, all right," Peter said, talking calmly to the colt. But there was something else about the big horse he could not name.

Peter always thought the colt was special. Riding Barbaro felt unlike riding any other two-year-old. Peter just couldn't find a word to describe it.

★ ★ ★ ★ ★ ★ ★ ★ ★ ★

Yes, the power and the stride of the colt were indeed impressive. And the colt was always balanced and willing. But that was not all Peter felt when aboard the rippling muscles and powerful frame. But what should he call it?

During these morning workouts, the trainer Michael Matz often rode a big chestnut beside Barbaro. As they headed up to the track together, he and Peter would agree, "No, we can't rush this. We just have to wait."

"Yes. He's not quite ready to do his real job yet. He's immature. We have to be patient."

Like Jill and John Stephens in Florida, they knew they needed to think of more than speed. The young horse's mental development was as important as his athletic growth. Like a kid in grade school, Barbaro sometimes had a hard time keeping his mind on what he was being asked to do.

On the racetrack he would look far off to his left. Then something would catch his attention on his right. Sometimes Barbaro's workout down the track looked like a worm's path. Sometimes moving in a straight line was no more important to him than sniffing an empty bucket.

After all, there were so many things to explore and check out! So many pretty fillies trotting up and down the track!

All the while, Peter Brette was thinking, *Something, yes. Something is very unusual here.*

★ ★ ★ ★ ★ ★ ★ ★ ★ ★ ★ ★ ★

After a few steps on the track, Peter signaled to the young colt to gallop. Barbaro settled into his cruising speed. The big colt's stride was enormous. He seemed to lift from the ground and float across it before touching down to take off again.

Peter felt the colt lift his knees higher than most horses. But the colt was balanced and efficient. There was no wasted motion.

The practice track was covered in wood chips. It made a surface similar to grass, or turf. But Barbaro didn't seem to care what he ran on.

After his morning workout Barbaro would come back to the barn, and Eduardo would give him a shower and hold him while he grazed. Eduardo also groomed him then, spending an hour polishing the colt's coat until it was the shiny brown of new shoes.

That first month, Peter asked Barbaro to run "two-minute licks," which meant to run a mile in two minutes, or one eighth of a mile in fifteen seconds. For a Thoroughbred, that's cruising speed, similar to a kid on a skateboard gliding around a curve. A mile in two minutes is twice as fast as the fastest man can run the same distance.

Barbaro seemed to think two-minute licks were no more difficult than a pasture romp. His head was always up, his ears pricked. He was eager to do whatever Peter told him to do.

★ ★ ★ ★ ★ ★ ★ ★ ★ ★ ★ ★ ★ ★

Soon Peter and Michael were ready to ask the big colt to "breeze" a furlong. A "furlong" is another term for one eighth of a mile, or 220 yards. That's about equal to two footballs fields. In racehorse language "breezing" means to speed up and *really* move. *Really, really move.* This wasn't going to be cruising.

Breezing would be a pace that asked the colt to exert himself. He would have to put forth much effort and energy. This was going to be a request for serious speed. No more fiddley-futzing around.

As Barbaro cruised down the track, Peter crouched low on his back. Peter shortened the reins. He signaled to the big colt to change gears. He squeezed with his legs, even though he was riding with short stirrups in jockey position. And he clucked with his tongue.

Immediately Barbaro stretched out, covering more ground. The sound of the colt's breathing became like a huge bellows now. It was an air pump, singing low. There was a huge intake of breath and then a push out. And Barbaro's breathing was timed perfectly with his soaring legs beneath his powerful body.

Saliva from the colt's mouth blew back against Peter's face. The sound of the colt's hooves on the track was like bongo drums.

At the next eighth-mile pole, Peter drew the colt back to a cruising gallop. "GREAT JUMPING

★ ★ ★ ★ ★ ★ ★ ★ ★ ★ ★ ★ ★

GARBANZO BEANS!" Peter cried. Barbaro didn't even seem to know they'd been breezing! For Barbaro, breezing was just another gallop. He didn't care either that he'd never heard "great jumping garbanzo beans" before. After all, humans sometimes said silly things. And "great jumping garbanzo beans" didn't sound like some kind of new command.

Back at the barn Eduardo showered Barbaro and put a blue blanket on him. He led him out onto the field to eat grass.

Peter came to hold the lead rope. He studied the big colt and felt the mystery of what he could not name.

Back in his stall, Barbaro lazed about in his morning routine. Only, now Dr. Anderson came with her equipment to check his breathing. She did this every time a horse was breezed in its workout. She checked to see if there were any problems in the horse's airways.

She used an endoscope, a narrow metal tube covered with rubber. She threaded it into Barbaro's nose, but it wasn't painful. It tickled like a straw being put up there. And the camera on the end sent a picture to a screen set up in the stall.

Dr. Anderson could see that Barbaro's airways were clear. Running at such great speed caused him no trouble. The next time he was asked for that speed, nothing would be in the way of his getting all the air he needed.

★ ★ ★ ★ ★ ★ ★ ★ ★ ★ ★ ★ ★ ★ ★

Dr. Anderson checked for muscle strains, too. She looked to see if Barbaro was dehydrated—without enough water in his body. As a quick way to test this, she pinched his skin into a little tent on his neck. If it took more than a second for the tent to go away, that meant there was not enough water in his body. But Barbaro was fine.

In every way, she looked after each horse as the important athlete it was becoming. And Barbaro was now ready to perform at very high levels.

All that summer the colt's workouts seemed like nothing to him. Breezing was no more than a few loops around the old Kentucky pasture, swapping off the lead with Last Best Place, playfully nipping whenever they got close. Most likely Last Best Place was at another training farm. No doubt Barbaro was remembering those foal days when they'd fallen in love with speed.

Soon Barbaro was breezing two furlongs. After a few more weeks he was breezing half a mile, and then five eighths of a mile. And each time Peter asked for more speed, Barbaro gave it. There would be that enginelike change of gear, the soaring feet, the bongo-drum of his hooves, the bellowslike breathing flaming the fire.

Together they danced to the beat of Barbaro's speed song. But as yet Barbaro did not have even a clue there was something beyond breezing. Racing speed for him

★ ★ ★ ★ ★ ★ ★ ★ ★ ★ ★ ★

was as unknown as a blank answer space in a math problem.

Then suddenly, after a workout, riding the big colt back to the barn, Peter knew how to describe what he had been feeling. *There's no end to him*, he said to himself. *No bottom to the well.*

Indeed, every time Peter asked Barbaro for more speed, the colt answered. It was as if Barbaro had no limit to how much speed he could give.

Was it really possible, then? Was the big colt like a deep well of water from which Peter could draw, on and on? Peter looked at the colt in wonderment and admiration. Rarely had he been atop such an athlete as this. The power was stunning.

Barbaro walked calmly up to the barn and stood quietly while Eduardo showered him. The colt was as casual and relaxed about his great abilities as a school-yard kid swinging from a high bar.

July came, and with it came a change in Barbaro.

His hips were now higher than his withers. He was like an earthquake in motion. All the growth plates in his body were expanding. He was growing so fast he was weak. He lost weight.

Simply, he was having a growth spurt. Peter Brette and Michael Matz knew to be especially patient now.

The colt's workouts were scaled down. He was

★ ★ ★ ★ ★ ★ ★ ★ ★ ★ ★ ★ ★ ★

exercised every day, but he was not asked for great speed. He was a masterpiece in the making. And as with all superb athletes, he had to come into his greatest abilities in his own time.

The question now was, how grand would he become? Would he grow too much and become clumsy? Would he still be as honest and willing to work? Would he find that eating and lazing around were more fun than flying? Would he forget to hear his speed song?

Always and forever, there was an unanswered question chasing Barbaro like Last Best Place in their pasture as foals: What would he really be?

★ ★ ★ ★ ★ ★ ★ ★ ★ ★ ★ ★ ★

★ CHAPTER 12 ★

Business Is Afoot

SEPTEMBER CAME, AND BARBARO'S growth spurt left him inches taller. He stood now at almost seventeen hands.

His muscles were hard and powerful. His bones were dense and strong. His coat was as shiny as a new leaf on a tree. He was magnificent. And he seemed to know it. He didn't brag exactly, but he *did* swagger a little. He walked with growing confidence. He was ready to be given a challenge.

Before all horses are raced, they have to pass a gate test. One morning a special instructor came to the training farm. This gate tester walked out to the starting gate, and Peter Brette swung up onto Barbaro. Eduardo led horse and rider toward the gate.

This was something Barbaro had seen and walked through many times. After all,

★ ★ ★ ★ ★ ★ ★ ★ ★ ★ ★

in Florida, before he'd turned two, John Stephens had taught Barbaro there was nothing to be afraid of in a starting gate.

The gate tester stood beside the line of gates mounted on wheels. Another man stood on a little ledge inside the gate. When Barbaro walked in, this man held Barbaro's head straight so he was looking out at the track. Always, in every race, there would be someone to do this.

Peter Brette spoke calmly to the colt. "You'll do this many times, big guy. No worry. No sweat."

Barbaro looked out at the empty track and pricked his ears.

The bell sounded. The gates flew open. Peter urged Barbaro with a squeeze. The colt leapt forward and galloped down the track. Barbaro now had a passing test score. It was certified that he could stand quietly and break cleanly.

Now he had to learn what a real race was like.

What would it be like to pass another horse in a race? How would Barbaro run when he learned what the game was about?

He needed to work a mile beside another horse who would fight for the lead. He needed to pass another horse who would dare him not to.

On a chilly morning in September, Peter Brette walked into Barbaro's stall carrying his race saddle and

★ ★ ★ ★ ★ ★ ★ ★ ★ ★ ★ ★ ★

bridle. Barbaro might have sensed some new, important business was afoot. He might have gotten a hint that something exciting was about to happen.

But then, Barbaro was not a human wanting to give words to everything. He understood only that a short brown filly was standing at the end of the shed row.

She began walking up to the training track. Her tail switched. She had a prissy little stride.

Peter Brette swung up onto Barbaro and headed after her.

The filly was plain, the color of dirt after a rain, and she had long floppy ears. But there was a keenness in her eyes. It said, *Don't fool with me. I mean business, big-time.*

Teresa, an exercise rider, was perched on the filly's back. The horse walked up to the practice track with a swish and a swagger. She almost pranced. She knew the track was not just for practice. She had run races. She had won. She knew about ripping speed from legs that had already run a half mile. She knew about the burn of lungs when they were asked for more air.

Barbaro followed, clueless but curious.

Michael Matz came up beside Barbaro and looked up at Peter. "Don't hang back," he warned. "This filly knows what this is all about. She'll be serious. If she gets too far ahead, Barbaro might not have a chance to catch up. And his confidence will be hurt."

★ ★ ★ ★ ★ ★ ★ ★ ★ ★ ★ ★ ★ ★

It was so necessary now that nothing damage Barbaro's courage. He had been signed up for his first real race. It was only a few weeks away.

A groom led Barbaro and the filly into the starting gate. No one else was on the track. The soil of the racing course was untouched.

A groom inside each gate held the horse's head forward, looking out.

The bell sounded.

The sharp burr almost startled Barbaro. He'd been admiring the filly's long ears. She'd been giving him a mean look too, like, *Who do you think you are, big guy?* She burst from the gate as though she'd heard a dinner bell. And Barbaro hurried to catch up.

Peter Brette felt Barbaro cruising along, running comfortably with little effort. He had his head right at the filly's hip bone, just following her around. They passed the one-eighth pole, then the two-eighths pole. Then the third pole. Right at Barbaro's nose the filly's powerful hindquarters churned, burning up the track. She was good at this.

For her this was all business. In fact, her feet were flying with determination, and she was aiming for the finish line as if she had a shopping coupon at a sweet feed store.

That's good. You're fine, Peter Brette said through all his signals to Barbaro. Barbaro's long stride was licking up the track. He was staying right at the filly's hip.

Four-eighths, five, six-eighths, seven.

And now Barbaro felt Peter Brette squeeze more and shorten his reins. The bit moved higher in Barbaro's mouth. He had something to lean on more steadily now. He balanced and reached. His neck lowered. His lungs expanded. His hindquarters coiled like a rabbit's.

Barbaro looked into the filly's eye and saw her daring him. For a moment he hesitated. She was a spunky thing. She had the same fire and teasing eyes that Last Best Place had had. And it would have been nice to just hang out with her and gallop for a while. But Peter was asking him to pass her. And Barbaro knew he was supposed to pay attention to Peter.

For only a second Barbaro hung in the air, undecided. Then he uncoiled, his powerful back legs reaching far up under his belly and thrusting him forward. Peter felt the colt lower his whole body. He was like a bird hunkering down to take flight. He simply flew over the length of the homestretch, beating the filly by ten lengths. She was left in the dust, disappointed but admiring of Barbaro too.

Now both Peter and Michael cried aloud, "GREAT JUMPING GARBANZO BEANS!"

Indeed, what words could describe such a horse? What kind of athlete might they have?

★ ★ ★ ★ ★ ★ ★ ★ ★ ★ ★ ★ ★

Now only one question was left. Would Barbaro do this in a real race? How would he run on a real track on a real race day? Would he be able to hear his speed song then?

No one could answer that until the actual moment came.

★ ★ ★ ★ ★ ★ ★ ★ ★ ★ ★ ★ ★ ★ ★

CHAPTER 13

Spooky October

BOTH THE BEAUTY OF HORSES AND their speed feed imaginations. Horses' bravery and strength linger in our minds. We like to put words to what we feel, like Peter trying to find a word for what he felt when riding Barbaro.

Thousands of years ago the earliest storytellers learned that people like to hear the same story over and over. They like it even when they know how the story ends.

These stories tell about things everyone discovers in life, at one time or another. We all long for stories that will guide us as we live in the world.

Storytellers found that when they put a horse in a story, it made the tale twice as engaging. Listeners were enchanted. Soon heroes in stories rode horses when they

★ ★ ★ ★ ★ ★ ★ ★ ★ ★ ★

killed dragons. Kings rode horses when they came before their subjects.

It was only a matter of time before these stories, called myths, became like cook pots. Facts and wishes swirled together. And horses took on magical powers.

One of the most famous magical horses was Pegasus. Thousands of years ago in Greece his story was created. He was born from a human. He had wings. He pawed the ground, and instantly a spring flowed. Everyone wanted to catch and ride the magical horse. Finally a prince named Bellerophon tamed him with a golden bridle. When Bellerophon became prideful and tried to ride Pegasus through the sky to Mount Olympus, where the Greek gods lived, Pegasus bucked and threw him off, leaving Bellerophon to wander hopelessly, hated by the gods. Pegasus found the stable on Olympus, where Zeus, king of the gods, saw him and took him to be his own steed. Zeus trusted Pegasus to bring him lightning and thunderbolts, which Zeus used to control his human subjects on Earth.

Horses have always stirred people's imaginations. Even a group of stars is named Pegasus. It is a constellation that shines brightest in the fall. And like that constellation, a lot of people thought Barbaro would shine brightest on the fourth day in October, the day of his first race.

★ ★ ★ ★ ★ ★ ★ ★ ★ ★ ★ ★

On October 3, Eduardo led Barbaro into a trailer. After a ride of only fifteen minutes, the trailer door opened and Eduardo led Barbaro down the ramp at the Delaware Park Racetrack. It was a beautiful old track with many trees. Barbaro walked around, looking at everything, and then he ate his supper in a stall deep with straw.

The next morning Peter jogged him around a little to give him time to look at a lot of strange things he had not seen before. For the first time he heard a crowd of people in a grandstand. He saw horses trotting everywhere with bright silk shirts on their jockeys.

At three o'clock the sky was as blue as a blue jay's wing. Clouds floated like melting marshmallows. Barbaro's owner, Gretchen Jackson, climbed the stairs in the grandstand and found her seat. Her husband, Roy, was at another racetrack watching another horse they owned.

Michael Matz saddled Barbaro. Peter stood in the paddock, watching, excited and nervous. Peter wanted Barbaro to show the world what he knew about the big colt. Yet no one can ever know how a young horse will act in a race. Some horses never find their courage to win.

The race jockey was now swinging up onto Barbaro. Peter walked up to him. "You're on the best horse here,"

★   ★   ★   ★   ★   ★   ★   ★   ★   ★   ★   ★   ★

Peter said. "He'll do anything you ask him to. When you're ready to let him *really* run, shake the reins at him. You'll never even have to raise your whip."

The jockey, José Caraballo, nodded and smiled. He was dressed in the blue, white, and green racing silks of the Jacksons' farm, Lael, which is a Gaelic word meaning "loyalty." That summed up the way the Jacksons felt about all their horses: They were loyal, always, to what was best for each horse. But many times Caraballo had heard trainers or exercise riders tell him something like what Peter had just said. Sometimes it had no more meaning than a wish.

Now race stewards began leading the horses to the starting gate. There were fourteen in the race. It was for a mile on turf. Peter headed to the grandstand. He wanted to watch the race on a TV screen in the hallway. That way he could see Barbaro up close as the horse turned for the homestretch.

Barbaro walked to the starting gate with his ears pricked, looking interested. Then suddenly he balked. It was like, *Uh-uh, I'm not going in there! That's downright spooky. Who says there's not a tiger hiding in the ceiling? Uh-uh, I ain't going. And you can't make me.*

Again and again he backed away from the starting gate. His eyes grew wide, and he shook his head. *Uh-uh. No way. Even if it's what you say—and there's not a real tiger in*

★ ★ ★ ★ ★ ★ ★ ★ ★ ★ ★ ★ ★ ★

there—then there's a ghost of a tiger in there. I'm not stupid. I'm not going to get trapped!

Seeing the problem, Peter sent word to Caraballo to take his feet out of the stirrups. Always when Peter rode Barbaro into the starting gate, he let his legs dangle against Barbaro's sides. It was a signal to relax and stop worrying. Peter could sense Barbaro's panic.

Caraballo dropped his legs. Barbaro recognized the signal and felt okay. He walked into the gate and stood while the steward inside held his head forward so he was looking out at the track. *Maybe the tiger will get that man! He'd make a better dinner for a tiger. Besides, if there is a tiger, I'm going to outrun him. He'll be left eating up the gate man and looking at my back!*

Barbaro's confidence was overcoming his fear.

The track looked a little like the track at home. It was grass, though. And there were those loud people along the rail. *But oh, well. Whatever. Whatever.*

Caraballo put his feet in the stirrups, ready. And then, *BRRRR.* The bell sounded.

Barbaro uncoiled into a leap. He was off down the track with his nose in the tail of a fat brown horse.

Two lengths ahead in the lead was another brown horse. None of the horses in the race were fillies. They were tough colts like Last Best Place. And they were

★ ★ ★ ★ ★ ★ ★ ★ ★ ★ ★ ★ ★ ★

running as if someone had yelled out, *Come and get it! Free pizza sweet feed!*

Barbaro galloped along. *Whatever. Whatever.* His speed song was not even turned on.

From inside the grandstand Peter watched Barbaro on the TV screen. In a close-up Peter could see the colt cruising. Barbaro still looked clueless. *Race? This is a race? No, this is a romp. If only that fat brown hotshot in front would quit fanning my face with his tail!*

Up in the grandstand Gretchen Jackson and Michael Matz nervously watched Barbaro, wondering how the colt would respond when Caraballo asked him for more speed.

At the three-eighths pole Caraballo signaled to Barbaro to switch leads. Barbaro in midstride swapped his right foreleg for his left. Now he was more balanced as he leaned into the turn. Then Caraballo asked him for more speed. Barbaro lowered into yet another gear. *Okay, okay. Whatever. Just get me back to that fancy stall in time for dinner.*

But Caraballo was wondering, would the big colt be ready to sprint in the homestretch?

Four-eighths. Five-eighths, six. Caraballo shortened the reins. He clicked with his tongue, *Now! Now! It's now or never.* He raised his whip, just in case the young horse did not answer.

★ ★ ★ ★ ★ ★ ★ ★ ★ ★ ★ ★ ★

But as Peter knew Barbaro would, the colt flattened. He lowered onto the turf like an engine revving, *RRRRRR. RRRRRR.* He reached into his deep well of speed and pulled out another gear. He coiled and uncoiled. He soared across the turf like Pegasus in his heavens.

Up in the grandstand Michael Matz and Gretchen Jackson nearly fell out of their seats. *GREAT JUMPING GARBANZO BEANS!* they all wanted to cry now, especially Caraballo, who was flying by the horse in the lead. If anyone did cry out, Barbaro was too busy to hear. He was soaring to his own music, his feet dancing to their own tune. He didn't even know the race was over. *Let's go. Let's go. There might be a sweet feed store right around that corner. Let's see. Let's see.* And then Caraballo was asking him to slow down. *Oh, gee!*

The show was over.

What show? Race? What race? Was that a race? How about an early supper?

Peter walked out of the grandstand to meet Barbaro. Peter smiled, thinking, *No, the colt still doesn't know what this is all about. He has no idea what great things he can accomplish.*

Gretchen Jackson walked down to the winner's circle. *Oh, how nice to win. It is always nice to win,* she was thinking. But she, like Barbaro, did not yet know they were at the beginning of a story to be written for all time.

★ ★ ★ ★ ★ ★ ★ ★ ★ ★ ★ ★ ★ ★

★ **CHAPTER 14** ★

Eyeball-to-Eyeball

BARBARO RAN A RACE ALMOST EVERY month after that. In November he was in Maryland. In December he went to Florida. There, in January, he ran a mile and an eighth, his longest race so far. All were on turf. And in all of the races he came in first.

In February he was taken to Gulfstream Park Racetrack near Miami, Florida, to run a race called the Holy Bull. This would be the first time he would run on dirt. "Let's try him," Michael Matz said. After all, everyone was eager to see how good Barbaro was.

But it rained the night before the race. The next morning, showers fell from the sky like water from a hose. The track wasn't just dirt now. It was slop. It was like a mud pie in a sandbox.

★　★　★　★　★　★　★　★　★　★

"Oh, he's not going to like having goo slung in his face," a lot of people said. Others declared, "He curls his legs too high. With his soaring stride, he'll be left in the mud like a bulldozer with a flat tire."

This race would be a real test for Barbaro. Up until now it had all been golden for him.

This time the famous jockey Edgar Prado would ride Barbaro for the first time. He was in the locker room putting on the blue, white, and green racing silks. Everyone in the racing world knew Prado. He had grown up in Peru and come to America as a teenager with the dream of being a jockey. Now he was one of the greatest jockeys in the sport.

Michael Matz saddled Barbaro. Gretchen and Roy Jackson climbed the stairs in the grandstand to find their seats.

Edgar Prado walked to the paddock. He wiped rain from his eyes and looked up at the big bay colt. Instantly he saw courage in Barbaro's eyes. Prado swung up into the saddle. He pulled down his goggles. He fastened his helmet.

Barbaro walked out onto the track. He was wearing new shoes. The day before, a farrier had nailed turn-down horseshoes onto all four of his hooves. It was a special way of putting an ordinary shoe on upside down, so the curl at the base would reach into the soil to grab it. Barbaro

★ ★ ★ ★ ★ ★ ★ ★ ★ ★ ★ ★ ★

trotted a little, feeling his new rider, and liking what he felt. Yes, this would be a good racing partner. The sloppy mud squished under his new shoes. *But so what?* He shook his head in the rain and aimed for the starting gate.

He walked in and stood calmly. He coiled. When the starting bell clanged, he leapt forward. His speed song started right away. *Running in the rain. Just running in the rain. Who says it's a bummer? There's nothing any funner.*

He passed the one-eighth pole, then the three-eighths. *My mama was a mudder. My papa could run even furder. Who said this was hard to do? Look out, I'm coming through!*

Five-eighths, six. *Slipping and sliding. Cruising and striding. Was told a long time ago I couldn't do this. I'd mess up and miss. But watch this!*

As if he were back in Kentucky as a foal, and he and Last Best Place were ripping around in a rain dance, Barbaro ran with glee. *Splish-splash, we're taking a bath.* The more that mud was slung in his face, the more he seemed to love it. This was like a food fight with goo! Then he felt Prado shake the reins and move his hands up, sending a hurry-up message. Aha! Now, this was going to be a cakewalk. Barbaro leaned into the bridle, reached into his well of speed, and pulled out another gear. He caught the lead horse and beat him by nearly a length.

Oh, it was a stunning race! Oh, it was as exciting

★ ★ ★ ★ ★ ★ ★ ★ ★ ★ ★ ★ ★ ★

as letting out a whole can of "GREAT JUMPING GARBANZO BEANS!"

"I can't believe it!" Gretchen Jackson exclaimed, running down the steps. "This is so incredible! I bet you, Roy, we're going to the Kentucky Derby."

Roy looked at her and shook his head. "Don't get your hopes up. We've been wanting a Derby horse for . . . how many years?"

"Oh, about thirty," Gretchen answered, laughing, pulling on a raincoat. "And this year we've got one! We're going. I can just feel it!" She handed Roy a raincoat too, and both of them hurried to the winner's circle.

Barbaro walked to meet them, rain pelting his face. Mud was in his ears. And up each leg was a stocking of slop. The mud was all over Prado, too. They were a team now, a pair who didn't care about rain, mud, hot, cold—any day at all was a good one for dipping into the well of speed. In the winner's circle Barbaro put his head up high; his ears were pricked. He looked magnificent. It was as if he knew he were every bit a winner. He'd shown those doubters. Gretchen Jackson saw the determination in his eyes. He was an athlete at the height of his power.

Yep, he was getting the hang of this racing game. He was on a roll.

People offered to buy him now. They offered a great

★ ★ ★ ★ ★ ★ ★ ★ ★ ★ ★ ★ ★ ★

deal of money. But Roy and Gretchen Jackson both said, "No way. This is a once-in-a-lifetime horse." Their dream of winning the Kentucky Derby was not for sale.

Barbaro was moved now to a training track nearby. He stayed there for two months, running everyday in workouts with Peter. Eduardo stayed to groom him and kept the young colt shining and happy. All Barbaro needed was somewhere to dance to his song. And then, on April first, he was entered in the Florida Derby, the biggest race at Gulfsteam Park, where he had won in the rain.

It was April Fools' Day. And the favorite horse, Sharp Humor, wanted to make Barbaro the fool.

The sun rose high. It was as round and yellow as an egg yolk. The sky looked like blue glass. The dirt track was dry.

Peter Brette worked Barbaro the morning of the race. They went for an easy gallop. And then Peter let Barbaro run hard for a short distance. Peter could feel how tuned Barbaro's muscles were; he had never been stronger. His speed song lay right under the surface, ready to explode into full sound.

Early in the afternoon Edgar Prado put on the blue, white, and green silks. John and Jill Stephens were there now, walking into the paddock to see the big bay they had trained as a yearling. Jill stood back, exclaiming, "Oh, my!"

★ ★ ★ ★ ★ ★ ★ ★ ★ ★ ★ ★ ★

John froze in admiration. He couldn't believe how much the young horse had changed. Barbaro looked different from every other horse there. John studied the big colt who wore a robe of confidence as if it were a royal cape. *This* was the athlete that had been waiting inside Barbaro to come out. *This* was the horse that could make history.

John and Jill climbed the stairs in the grandstand. They were so excited they could hardly sit. One of their kids, one of their students, was about to perform on an enormous stage. The yearling they'd known was about to reveal to the world an amazing talent, one they had helped him find within himself.

Barbaro coiled in the starting gate. He looked out at the track. There were eleven horses in the race. He was in post position number ten. That far away from the rail, he would have to take more steps than the others around the first turn.

The gate handler held his head, and then released. *BRRRR*, the buzzer sounded. Barbaro uncoiled and leapt out. His rival, Sharp Humor, took the lead. Sharp Humor was a dark bay horse, almost black, and he was as determined as Last Best Place heading to the barn for dinner. Barbaro wanted to reach over and nip his old friend for fun. But Sharp Humor was not Last Best Place. And this was a serious race. A *very* serious race.

★　★　★　★　★　★　★　★　★　★　★　★　★

This was the pathway to the Kentucky Derby. This was a chance to make history.

Barbaro dug in. He reached into his well of speed and turned up the volume. He heard the drumbeat of tigers in Africa, the beating wings of eagles, the roaring of engines powering silver bodies of planes. He dipped again and again into his well of speed. He hung just off the right shoulder of Sharp Humor.

At the turn for home, Prado let Barbaro edge closer. He asked for the lead switch. Barbaro answered. He came head-to-head with Sharp Humor. The dark bay leader looked Barbaro in the eye. Barbaro thought he was saying, *Isn't this a blast? Let's just hang here and cruise around. Let's just party hardy like two dudes on a prairie.*

For a moment Barbaro was duped. It *did* seem Barbaro wanted no more than to run with a pal. He and Sharp Humor were eyeball-to-eyeball. And Barbaro's memories of being back in Kentucky with Last Best Place seemed as present as the warm sun on his back and Edgar Prado prodding him.

Then suddenly Barbaro felt Prado swat him with the racing whip. *Oh, my!* Yet Barbaro remembered what Jill had taught him, back in his early days in Florida. The whip was a gesture. It was a way of talking with hands. And it sure caught Barbaro's attention. *Come on, now,* the whip was saying, *this is business. This isn't play. Pass him! Pass the dark teasing colt. He's not wanting to play. He's daring you! Let him see your heels!*

Well, okay, if you insist. Suddenly Barbaro understood how he'd misread the dark bay leader. Sharp Humor had been daring him to pass. *Okay. Okay. I see now. Yep, he was trying to make a fool of me. Dadgummit! So watch this!*

The speed well opened. Barbaro reached in. He soared past Sharp Humor to cross the finish line first.

Barbaro had won! He'd won his first really big race. It had been close, but he'd run the mile and one eighth in one minute and forty-nine seconds. Not bad for a colt who just wanted to hang out.

Peter Brette rushed from the grandstand to meet Barbaro on the way to the winner's circle. It was as if the colt had gone into the race as a boy and come out as a man. Peter looked up into Barbaro's eyes. Barbaro looked back.

Those eyes wore the look of a winner in every way now.

Kentucky Derby, here we come!

★ ★ ★ ★ ★ ★ ★ ★ ★ ★ ★ ★ ★

CHAPTER 15

Six-and-a-Half Lengths in Kentucky

FOR FIVE WEEKS BARBARO WOULD not run another race. "He'll get lazy," people said. Others said, "He won't be ready for the Kentucky Derby. This is a *big* mistake."

But Peter Brette and Michael Matz knew Barbaro's speed song did not need tuning. It was ready to be heard whenever he listened. All he needed was to be kept happy and exercised.

And happy was easy. Fourteen quarts of sweet feed a day. Unlimited timothy hay. That spelled H-A-P-P-I-N-E-S-S for Barbaro.

Rather than having Barbaro ride in a trailer all the way to Kentucky, the Jacksons decided he should fly. Eduardo led him

★ ★ ★ ★ ★ ★ ★ ★ ★ ★

onto a plane and helped fix a box stall deep with straw. Eduardo stayed with him too.

After landing at an airport in Kentucky, Barbaro and Eduardo met a waiting van. Barbaro rode it to the Keeneland racetrack, where Eduardo again made him feel at home in a big box stall. Here he stayed for four weeks. It was close to Churchill Downs, where he would run the Kentucky Derby, but not so close that he couldn't stay relaxed. Peter was here too. And every day, Barbaro and Peter trained just as always, just as if they were home, and not as if something special were about to happen.

To Barbaro those days felt just like any other days: any other place, any other stable with lots of other horses. He had no idea he was about to run the most important race in America. Sometimes he saw a horse that reminded him of that filly with the floppy ears—the one he'd run his practice race with, more than half a year ago now. Sometimes he thought he saw a horse like Last Best Place. Was his friend running a race somewhere too?

Nine days before the Kentucky Derby, Eduardo led Barbaro into a trailer to be driven to the famous racetrack at Churchill Downs. The grandstand was huge. The stables were fancy and big. As Eduardo led him into his new box stall, Barbaro seemed to say, *Whatever, whatever. Just make sure there's plenty to eat.*

Churchill Downs was so famous everyone almost

★ ★ ★ ★ ★ ★ ★ ★ ★ ★ ★ ★ ★

tiptoed around in it. The racetrack had a long and interesting history. The first race run there had been one hundred and thirty years before, and two freed slaves had won it. The trainer had been an African American, and so had the jockey. And now Barbaro had a chance to join all the horses who had trotted to the winner's circle for wreaths of roses to be laid around their necks.

Might he be one of the greats who have lived on as legends—along with War Admiral, Whirlaway, Citation, Secretariat, and Seattle Slew?

In the background of Barbaro's family, his great-great-grandfather Nashua had come in second in the Kentucky Derby to the winner, Swaps. But what about the distance? Could Barbaro keep up his great speed the whole way? He'd never raced a mile and a quarter. Would his well of speed be deep enough?

Most of the winners ran the distance in little more than two minutes. The great Secretariat was one of the few to win in less than two minutes. Could Barbaro be among those greats?

Every morning he exercised on the track, just as he would at home. And then, days before the race, the Jacksons drew post position number eight for him. Twenty horses would run the race altogether. It would be one of the largest and best fields of three-year-olds ever to run for the roses.

★ ★ ★ ★ ★ ★ ★ ★ ★ ★ ★ ★ ★

On that Thursday before the Saturday race, Peter breezed Barbaro, letting him touch the rim of the well of his great speed. In every way Barbaro felt ready.

The night before the race Peter opened the door to Barbaro's stall and quietly went in. He reached up and rubbed the colt's forehead. Barbaro looked calm and determined. His eyes were serene and confident. At birth, character traits lie hidden. Barbaro's great size and ability had been promised in his breeding, but until now no one could have seen his heart. Peter patted the great horse and thought of his own child, Nicholas, only three, and hoped his son would grow up to have the same character traits as Barbaro: his kindness, his honesty, his courage.

The next day Gretchen and Roy Jackson climbed the stairs into the grandstand. All the ladies were wearing hats. Some had wide brims and flowers and bows, in bright colors that made them seem like a field of flowers, bobbing and swaying as the spectators sat down.

The crowd, more than 150,000, was one of the largest in the racetrack's history. Everyone wanted to see this superhorse named Barbaro, who had never been defeated. He was one of only six in history to come to the Kentucky Derby without having lost a race. And he'd won most of his races by many lengths.

Back at Barbaro's training farm in Maryland, the

★ ★ ★ ★ ★ ★ ★ ★ ★ ★ ★ ★ ★

staff rented a big-screen TV and invited all their friends for a party. By post time, nearly two hundred people were crowded around the TV to cheer on the horse they knew so well.

In the famous paddock at Churchill Downs, Michael Matz saddled Barbaro and held the lead rope to the bridle. Edgar Prado walked from the jockey's locker room and swung up. Prado guided Barbaro to the starting gait.

Barbaro went in and stood quietly. All the while, his speed song was humming. It was traveling up into his legs, spreading through his shoulders, firing his hips with enormous power, singing unbeatable courage in his mind. The gate handler held Barbaro's head, keeping him straight and looking out at the track. And then *BRRRR!* The starting bell sounded. The gates swung open.

Barbaro leapt out. But as he did, his toe caught on the dirt and he stumbled. He went down almost to his knees.

Prado might have wanted to yell, *Yikes! We've got trouble!* But he was too busy hanging on.

Barbaro struggled for his stride, then found it. Right away he soared into second gear to catch up to the fourth horse behind the leader. In front a colt named Keyed Entry was burning up the track like a rabbit hustling from a hunter. And Keyed Entry was right. The whole field was after him.

★ ★ ★ ★ ★ ★ ★ ★ ★ ★ ★ ★ ★

Never before had Barbaro been with such determined colts! All were as tough and courageous as Last Best Place. And there were so many of them! It was like a traffic jam on a freeway heading to a feed store. But Prado wasn't really worried. He was feeling now the great reserve of speed in Barbaro's well. When he asked for it, he knew Barbaro would reach down in. He put Barbaro in stalking position behind the leaders and waited.

Heading around the turn, Prado asked Barbaro for a lead change. Barbaro switched in midair and accelerated. At the beginning of the homestretch, Prado shook the reins and shortened them. Barbaro lowered onto the track and pulled out his greatest speed yet. *GREAT JUMPING GARBANZO BEANS!* Prado could have cried, *He's taking off like a rocket!*

Indeed, it seemed Barbaro had sprouted wings to soar above the ground. He took the lead in the far turn. He sprinted ahead three lengths at the mile pole.

With only a furlong to go, Barbaro was running ahead by four lengths. And still his speed song was singing with plenty of notes and air.

He was all alone out in front now. He was running for the sheer love of running. He himself had never been big on this beat-a-friend thing. He ran for the sheer joy of it.

By the time Barbaro crossed the finish line, he was

★ ★ ★ ★ ★ ★ ★ ★ ★ ★ ★ ★ ★

six-and-a-half lengths in front of the next horse. No horse in the last sixty years had won the Kentucky Derby by such a great distance; the last time there had been a margin of victory this large was in 1946. Barbaro ran the last quarter mile in twenty-four-and-a-half seconds too—the most powerful finish since Triple Crown winner Secretariat in 1973.

Edgar Prado stood up in the stirrups, waving his arms, encouraging the cheers. The crowds in the grandstand were on their feet. Here was a new champion. And not just any champion but a horse of magnificent power. This was the one who could win the next two famous races to claim the Triple Crown.

Gretchen Jackson watched her horse gallop to a stop and trot back toward the winner's circle. She looked around at the great number of people cheering him, loving him for his ability and magnificence. The sound of their applause and amazement rose like a cloud of delight, hanging over the grandstand. Barbaro was a new hero. Everyone now saw how exceptional he was.

Gretchen turned to Roy. "You know what?" she whispered. "Barbaro no longer belongs to only us. He belongs to the people. He's America's horse. Listen. Can you hear how much they love him?"

Roy stood still, thinking. Around him the cheering did not stop or grow quieter. He nodded. Yes, just as

★ ★ ★ ★ ★ ★ ★ ★ ★ ★ ★ ★ ★

his wife had predicted months before that they would be here and might win, she was right again. Barbaro was more than *their* horse. He was on his way to becoming a legend.

They hurried to the winner's circle. Barbaro was already waiting. His head was up, his ears pricked.

He was looking quite majestic.

★ ★ ★ ★ ★ ★ ★ ★ ★ ★ ★ ★ ★ ★ ★

★ CHAPTER 16 ★

The Misstep No One Anticipated

BARBARO WAS NOW SO FAMOUS THAT reporters followed him. Newspapers, magazines, television—everyone wanted a story about Barbaro. Every day reporters waited at the training farm back in Maryland, where he was taken to get a little rest.

Reporters followed him to the practice track on the hill. They wanted to hear what he ate, and how he spent his days, and how fast he worked.

Barbaro ate through it all—caring only that all fourteen quarts of sweet feed fell into his bucket each day. He watched for his hay net to be full of that sweet timothy stuff that smelled as good as wild clover. Or rather, like a whiff of cookies to a human. To him it was the next best thing to spring

★ ★ ★ ★ ★ ★ ★ ★ ★ ★ ★

grass. And he ran on the practice track as joyfully as if he were passing Last Best Place in a play race.

Each day, he was turned out to relax and graze. Eduardo groomed him, just as he had before Barbaro had become a star. Peter was always there too, riding him, tuning his muscles, and keeping his speed song within hearing range. Almost everyone felt sure Barbaro would be the next Triple Crown winner. After all, he had won all six of his races so easily.

But now he had only two weeks before his next race. He barely had time to catch his breath. The Preakness, the next in the Triple Crown, was the longest distance yet—a mile and three sixteenths. No one knew if Barbaro's well of speed was deep enough for that.

On the day before the race Eduardo led Barbaro into a trailer. For an hour and a half they rode to Baltimore, Maryland, to the Pimlico Race Course. There, Eduardo walked him down the ramp and led him to a stall with deep, soft straw. His supper of sweet feed and hay was waiting just as it should have been. *Thank you, and what about seconds?* And in the morning Peter cruised Barbaro around the track so he could stretch his legs.

The morning was sunny. But every once in a while the sky would darken as though it were going to rain. Blustery wind blew. Then it would die down, and the sun would come out again, and the rain held off. It was

★ ★ ★ ★ ★ ★ ★ ★ ★ ★ ★ ★ ★

as if the weather were foretelling the outcome of the day.

Barbaro sensed something big was about to happen. People were everywhere. Reporters stood by, writing down every move he made. Television cameras followed him as if he were a rock star with a number one album. *All this fuss. And what for?* He was just a horse with a speed song, loving the music. Throw in a little alfalfa, and he was as happy as a moose in a cornfield.

Back at the training farm in Maryland the staff huddled again around a television set. Through the Kentucky Derby two hundred of them had cheered for him, and they felt they might have been his lucky charm. So they all gathered to cheer him on again.

In the afternoon Prado pulled on the blue, white, and green racing silks. For him it certainly did not feel like an ordinary race day. This was like standing on a stair, knocking on the door of history. It was just that the story he and Barbaro would write would not be the one he'd expected. Their legend had other plans for them.

Michael Matz held Barbaro's bridle. He tested the girth on the saddle. Yes, it was tight enough. Prado swung up. Barbaro walked calmly toward the starting gate.

Peter and his family, with Gretchen and Roy Jackson, waited in the grandstand, excited and ready to watch. They

★ ★ ★ ★ ★ ★ ★ ★ ★ ★ ★ ★ ★

were hoping Barbaro would be able to reach deep into his well of speed in order to last through the long distance of a mile and three sixteenths.

Then, after only a moment in the starting gate, Barbaro burst through. And Prado was saying through the reins, *Look, kiddo, you've jumped the gun. This is not the race yet. Whoa!*

The second time, Barbaro got it right and burst out of the starting gate along with the other three-year-olds. Right away he turned on his speed song. It was as if he now knew this was history. This was his destiny, his breeding, his life. Everything Prado was telling him was signaling the importance of this day and this race. Even though that morning Peter had kept him relaxed and cruising, the significance of the day had come through. *Now is the time. Write your name in the history books. Write the legend of your speed where the music will be heard forever.*

And then, bam! That step. That horrible misstep. The back right ankle had turned. And then shattered. *What? Why?* And now Prado was jumping off and telling Barbaro to be still.

Barbaro looked at Prado. With all of the horse language he knew, he pleaded, *Help me. Help me out, here. I don't understand.*

Outriders reached him, galloping fast. They stood to direct the race, still going on. And since the field

★ ★ ★ ★ ★ ★ ★ ★ ★ ★ ★ ★

of horses had started behind where they would need to cross the finish line—to equal the mile and three sixteenths—Barbaro would be in the way of the end of the race!

An ambulance pulled onto the track. Dr. Palmer, a veterinarian sitting in the stands, ran to join the racetrack veterinarian. Both of them now were reaching Barbaro. They gave him a painkiller, and Dr. Palmer bent down to put a splint on the broken leg. Barbaro seemed to understand. He stood still. It was as if he wanted to help.

Outriders formed a line, showing the oncoming field of horses where to go. All the horses in the race were now sprinting for the finish line. The outriders led them between the rail and the ambulance, while also sheltering Barbaro. In the midst of so much activity, the outriders created a sense of calm.

Eduardo and Peter Brette rushed to Barbaro. And Michael Matz and the Jacksons ran from their seats and were now on the track. Gretchen looked up into the eyes of her magnificent horse. She was as stunned by the tragic misstep as he was. But even now, with such great disappointment, Barbaro stood majestically.

The veterinarians led Barbaro into the ambulance. Eduardo got in beside him. He knew Barbaro was confused, and he was not about to let his friend ride off

★ ★ ★ ★ ★ ★ ★ ★ ★ ★ ★ ★ ★ ★ ★

without him. The ambulance was too high for Gretchen to reach up to say what she wanted to say to Eduardo. He might not understand her English, anyway. Instead, as the doors were closing, she reached in and kissed Eduardo's hand to show her gratitude.

Back at the barn, X-rays of Barbaro's broken leg were quickly taken and e-mailed to Dr. Kathy Anderson at the training farm. She, with all the others, had seen the misstep on TV and was silent and stunned. Instantly she e-mailed the X-rays to the surgeon at the New Bolton Center at the University of Pennsylvania School of Veterinary Medicine. But Dr. Dean Richardson was in Florida, operating on another horse. As soon as he could, he caught a plane home.

Now Eduardo was riding in the ambulance with Barbaro to the hospital. Eduardo was petting him, talking soothingly in Spanish. Over and over, Barbaro heard the Spanish word for horse, *"Caballo, caballo.* Good, good, *caballo."* Eduardo would not leave him. Barbaro trusted him. Eduardo had been with him through every step of his racing career.

Behind the ambulance a line of cars followed. Barbaro was speeding toward the Pennsylvania hospital with police cars clearing the way. Overhead, a helicopter with cameras followed mile for mile.

At each overpass high above the highway, people

gathered, rushing to be there after seeing the horrible misstep on television or hearing about it on the radio. Banners flew. GOOD LUCK, BARBARO. PRAY FOR BARBARO.

People waved and held up signs and posters. WE LOVE YOU, BARBARO. WE'RE PULLING FOR YOU, BARBARO. DON'T GIVE UP, BARBARO.

Inside the ambulance Barbaro put his muzzle in Eduardo's hand and shook his head against the pain. When he got wherever he was going, he hoped there'd be endless buckets of sweet feed. And with some aspirin in it.

At the hospital Gretchen and Roy pulled up behind the ambulance and got out in time to see their magnificent horse back out, and then cleverly turn. As Eduardo led him, Barbaro made up a three-legged hop down the ramp and into the hospital. And as he did, Gretchen and Roy saw every bit of their horse's intelligence and confidence still there.

It was as if Barbaro were saying, *Don't count me out. It'll take more than this to be the end of me.*

What he did not know was that no horse had ever lived through such a grave injury. With horses there is always the risk of infection after surgery, and the risk of other complications that humans don't have to worry about if they break a leg. But while to everyone else the accident seemed devastating, to Barbaro it was just a

★   ★   ★   ★   ★   ★   ★   ★   ★   ★   ★   ★   ★

race cut short. His speed music had been turned off midsong. He had a different race to run now. He had *surviving* on his mind. It was his challenge to find the new music.

★ ★ ★ ★ ★ ★ ★ ★ ★ ★ ★ ★ ★ ★ ★

CHAPTER 17

Wrinkled Brows and Bottomless Buckets

THE DAYS TOOK ON A NEW RHYTHM. Barbaro's yearling days seemed to be circling back in a chorus. Only now instead of having a slight injury, his life hung like a leaf in a cold wind. It could blow off at a sudden change of direction. And the wrinkled brows above the eyes that studied him every minute told him it would take all his courage to hang on.

That first night Eduardo, with a nurse showing them the way, led him straight into a special part of the horse hospital. Here in the intensive care unit someone would give him care every hour, all through the night. Right away a veterinarian put a line in a vein in Barbaro's neck to give him saline—water with salt in it. It was

★ ★ ★ ★ ★ ★ ★ ★ ★ ★ ★

especially important that he not get dehydrated during the night.

Over the years equine surgeons had learned that a horse's body needs time to adjust to a bad injury. It's best not to perform surgery right after a trauma. So it was okay that Dr. Richardson was not there that first night. He would have waited to operate anyway.

Just as Barbaro had hoped, his feed bucket was filled. And it was good, sweet grain too. He ate voraciously. He ate as fast as a vacuum cleaner sucking up Cheerios. Then he lay down.

Several times throughout the night he got up. Then he would lie down again. And each time he got up, people looked in at him, amazed. Barbaro found he could do a whole lot on three legs. He was as skillful as a ballet dancer doing twirls on the tip of a toe.

Eagerly, through the top rails of his stall, he looked out at the staff who came to look in at him. They marveled at how well he was doing. But it was as if Barbaro were thinking, *So what? So what? Just keep the buckets coming. And where's the hay? I thought you said there'd be more hay.*

And soon there was.

But as the hour came nearer to when he would be operated on, the food stopped. It was best for his stomach to be empty when he was anesthetized for the surgery.

★ ★ ★ ★ ★ ★ ★ ★ ★ ★ ★ ★ ★ ★

In the morning everyone was relieved to see how lively Barbaro was. It was going to take more than a broken leg to steal his strength. And especially his appetite.

Near noon Dr. Richardson led Barbaro into the operating room. A table with its surface set vertically was moved next to the big bay colt, and as Barbaro was given an anesthetic to put him to sleep, the table took Barbaro's weight and flipped up so that it was horizontal with Barbaro on it. And there he was at waist level so the surgeons could work on him.

For more than five hours Dr. Richardson carefully rebuilt the three bones that had shattered in Barbaro's leg. Dr. Richardson used screws and plates made of bone. Twenty-seven screws in all. Then, to give the leg a lot of protection, a cast was put on Barbaro's leg all the way over his hock—the part that is like the human knee.

The greatest threat now was infection. When Dr. Richardson walked out of the operating room, he knew that Barbaro had as much chance of living as a coin had of landing on heads after being flipped in the air. Barbaro's life was indeed as fragile as that leaf hanging in the wind. And no one could predict the outcome.

One of the greatest dangers was how Barbaro would wake up from the surgery. Waking up from being put into such a deep sleep is risky for a horse. Coming out

★ ★ ★ ★ ★ ★ ★ ★ ★ ★ ★ ★ ★ ★

of anesthesia, a horse loses his sense of direction. He doesn't know where he is or what is happening. And he panics. Another famous horse, Ruffian, who broke her leg in a race, thrashed about so much after surgery that she hurt herself even more and had to be put down. From her, equine doctors learned that it's best for a horse to wake up in water, that it's best for a horse to be cushioned as it struggles.

Dr. Richardson often said that failures teach us what we need to know. Over the years, he and other equine doctors had learned a great deal, especially from Ruffian. So the hospital had built a recovery pool.

Blindfolded, Barbaro was put into a sling and lowered into the deep, warm water and onto a rubber raft, where his legs could hang through. He would gallop in the water until he slowly woke up. Dr. Richardson stood by, wearing a helmet in case Barbaro thrashed and struck him with a hoof as he came out of the recovery pool. Barbaro woke up as though he were swimming. He couldn't see because of the blindfold. So he didn't panic as a pulley, run by a motor, lifted him high out of the water and swung him over onto the floor. He stood and shook himself off.

Dr. Richardson led him back to his stall. And everyone gathered around, eager to see how Barbaro would do.

By suppertime Barbaro was moving around in his

★ ★ ★ ★ ★ ★ ★ ★ ★ ★ ★ ★ ★ ★

stall, sleepy but hungry, and wanting to know, *Where're the groceries? Who's going to sling the hash? It's four o'clock, hurry and bring the grub!*

Oh yes, the cafeteria in this place was good.

Seemingly bottomless buckets of sweet feed appeared. And carrots. Everyone seemed to have a treat for him. And his stall was already being decorated with get-well cards and messages.

But why so many wrinkled brows? Always so many wrinkled brows.

Barbaro looked through the top of his stall, not understanding the dangers he faced. There was always the chance he could develop an infection in his broken leg. But also, with his putting so much weight on his good rear leg—the left one—would it develop a problem too? If so, it would be like that old saying—he wouldn't have a leg to stand on! And if that happened, Barbaro's life would be threatened even more.

On the sixth day after the surgery a farrier came to the hospital to make a special shoe for the hoof of Barbaro's good back leg. The farrier glued it onto the endangered left hind hoof. He lay Barbaro down while he did this so Barbaro wouldn't have to stand on his broken leg in the cast.

Every care was taken to protect Barbaro from the next big threat.

★　★　★　★　★　★　★　★　★　★　★　★　★

On May 30, ten days after his tragic misstep, Barbaro heard a familiar voice. He turned around from where he was eating hay in the corner of his stall and saw the familiar face and the familiar walk—the way Edgar Prado came into his stall and touched him in his old way. Rubbing the heart on his forehead, patting the soft muzzle that Barbaro liked to place in Prado's hand, here was Barbaro's best racing partner. Barbaro playfully nipped the hand and nuzzled the shoulder.

Prado wasn't wearing racing silks now. He wore a surgical gown and covers on his shoes. His brow was wrinkled too. And then he smiled, revealing his thoughts, *If tears could heal you, you'd be well by now.*

Barbaro bent his knees, folded his front legs, and lowered himself onto the deep straw bedding for a nap. Prado knelt and scooted around so he was close to Barbaro. And as Barbaro felt his racing partner next to him, he lifted his head and put it in Prado's lap.

Bottomless buckets. Yep, they're real nice. But so is a warm safe place for a nap.

Barbaro had always put his trust in people. And now, more than ever, that trust was his strength.

★ ★ ★ ★ ★ ★ ★ ★ ★ ★ ★ ★ ★

CHAPTER 18

The Eyes Have It

DAYS PASSED. AND BARBARO LEARNED to move to his new music. There was only a box stall for him to shuffle around in now. But moving was so difficult he didn't need much space. Besides, the cast was as big as a caveman's club and about as handy if he wanted to swat a fly. But there weren't many flies here. And anyway, Barbaro had plenty of people fretting over him, ready to brush away a fly if one did slip in.

Sixteen hundred reporters stopped by at one time or another to wait outside for word on how Barbaro was doing. He got more than fifty thousand e-mails from well-wishers. Every day baskets of carrots arrived, or posters, or get-well cards.

No one was allowed into the ICU without special clothes and special covers on his or her shoes. No one wanted to carry

★ ★ ★ ★ ★ ★ ★ ★ ★ ★ ★

in a germ that could harm Barbaro. Every day Gretchen Jackson came to see him. Michael Matz and Peter came too. Outside Barbaro's stall the rubber floor was washed in chemicals to kill any stray germs. Everyone worried that Barbaro's leg would become infected.

Then on June 13 he was anesthetized again and his cast was changed. His leg looked excellent. Barbaro was making history again. It looked as though he would live through this. He might be the first horse to recover from such a badly broken leg.

But as June moved into July, the music took on sour notes and the rhythm changed. No longer did the day sing a quiet chorus of *Wait, wait, wait.* Pain now ran from Barbaro's legs up into his shoulders and hips and neck and head. His ears flopped. His head drooped. Buckets of food were no longer as exciting. Hay didn't look so good either. It was clear he was working hard to stay still and wait.

Again he was anesthetized, and his cast was cut off. Two bent screws were found and replaced. Three new ones were added. But that didn't solve the problems. Barbaro was still troubled. Two days later he was anesthetized again and a plate was replaced as well as many more screws. A small abscess was found on the sole of his left, uninjured hoof. This was very worrisome. Was his good leg developing the trouble everyone had feared?

★ ★ ★ ★ ★ ★ ★ ★ ★ ★ ★ ★ ★ ★

A longer cast was put on in the hopes that it would give him more support. But the new cast did not work. Barbaro could not stand on the leg any better than before. It was taken off and a shorter one was put back on. Dr. Richardson said there were some tough days ahead. Wrinkled brows deepened. Barbaro's mind music became jarring and out of tune.

During all the long hours on the operating table, Barbaro had sweated a lot, and his right hip had become blistered. It lost hair. His coat on that hip became splotched with white dots because the roots of his hair had gone numb. Waking up in the recovery pool had been hard on his tail, too. Long hairs were pulled out by the weight of the water as he galloped awake, and his tail was now no longer than a dust mop.

But what are looks compared with living each day and looking forward to bottomless buckets of sweet feed and hay? Barbaro didn't give a fat hello about how long his tail was. After all, white dots on his hip could look like polka-dot pajamas. And if he was growing as thin as a scarecrow in a cornfield, his feet were thanking him for not having to hold up extra pounds. Besides, he *was* a scarecrow—shooing away the threats that could circle down to whisk away his life.

And then in the middle of July, on the night of the twelfth day, what everyone had feared might happen

★ ★ ★ ★ ★ ★ ★ ★ ★ ★ ★ ★ ★

happened. Barbaro's good left hind leg gave way. Bearing so much weight on it, his hoof wall—which is like a fingernail on a person—separated from the bones underneath. In horseman's language, he had foundered. It's a condition known as laminitis. Barbaro's greatest danger was now here, threatening to stop the music forever.

Gretchen and Roy Jackson rushed to be with him. Michael Matz did too. Peter and Eduardo held their breaths and silently waited to hear word of their dear Barbaro. Gretchen and Roy thought about letting the doctors put Barbaro down. The sight of him in so much pain was almost too much to bear. Barbaro would hardly eat at all. His ears flopped and his head drooped.

But when Gretchen and Roy and Michael Matz and Dr. Richardson walked into his stall to make this hard, hard decision, Barbaro lifted his head and looked back at them, eye to eye. There in his gaze was a certain light.

Only someone who has known an animal a long time and in many circumstances knows what that moment feels like. An animal who is beloved speaks to its caretakers in ways that are very much like music. And Barbaro seemed to be singing, *I won't give up if you won't.* His eyes had the desire to live.

He showed every bit of the courage he had always shown, only now his race was not on a racetrack but living through each day.

★   ★   ★   ★   ★   ★   ★   ★   ★   ★   ★   ★

"Let's go on," Gretchen Jackson said. "If the doctors can control his pain, let's go on."

Roy nodded. "If he's not ready to give up, we can't."

Dr. Richardson walked to his desk and began plotting a new plan of treatment. The days ahead would not be easy. But Barbaro deserved every effort that everyone could make.

He was at the starting gate again of a new and desperate race.

★ ★ ★ ★ ★ ★ ★ ★ ★ ★ ★ ★ ★ ★

★ CHAPTER 19 ★

Belonging to the World

DR. RICHARDSON ADMINISTERED A strong medicine to kill the pain. The medicine was sent into Barbaro's back. Given through a tube, it was released in small amounts all day and through the night. Again Barbaro was taken to the operating room and anesthetized and flipped up onto the table so the surgeons could work on him.

Almost all of his dead hoof was cut away so a new hoof could grow back. But growing a new hoof is not an easy or a quick thing. Growing one could take six months, maybe more. And the hoof needed to come back solid and strong.

A sling was placed in his stall so he could spend part of the day in it, resting.

★ ★ ★ ★ ★ ★ ★ ★ ★ ★

His appetite came back, and he neighed when he heard the feed cart coming down the hall. He whinnied for more hay and reached for the carrots the nurses held through the top of his stall.

The old Barbaro was back, and the light in his eyes was now a bonfire, fueled by the promise of every day. The ICU was filled with company, too. There was a foal whose mother had accidentally stepped on it. There was a sick sheep, whom the nurses carried around in a wheelbarrow. A sick alpaca was a few stalls down. A pygmy goat and its baby were close by. The baby was no bigger than a tiny terrier dog. Barbaro could hear it bleat for this, and call for that. Its bleating sounded like a horn on a riding lawn mower. And more than one mare who was having trouble carrying her foal long enough to be born nickered through the stall doors.

Each patient was getting better. Each was getting around-the-clock care.

If Barbaro could have sung aloud, he could have made up his own verses to "Old MacDonald Had a Farm." Certainly there were enough different animal voices to fill in the sounds: *With a baaa-baaa here, and a neigh-neigh there, and a bleat-bleat here, and a whinny-whinny there.*

But that alpaca—he didn't bother to even bleat. He

★ ★ ★ ★ ★ ★ ★ ★ ★ ★ ★ ★ ★

sucked in his lips and said nothing. He spit at the nurses, though.

And all of the animals at dinnertime sang loud and clear in their own voices: *Hurry up with the grub!*

With the sling in his stall now, Barbaro learned he could go stand next to it when he was tired, and someone would help him get into it. He'd always been pretty good at bossing people around.

The governor of Pennsylvania came to see him. The president of the university did too.

If the hospital had allowed in every visitor who'd wanted to see him, there wouldn't have been room to stand. Posters and cards and letters changed on his stall every week. Outside the hospital, banners offered well wishes. GROW, HOOF, GROW, one said, since now time was the only medicine that could heal Barbaro.

If his new hoof grew in strong, he would be allowed to leave the hospital and live more the way a horse likes to live. There might not be romping in a pasture as he once had done as a foal, but he would have a good, fun life with many human friends to spend the days with.

By the middle of summer Barbaro was walking out into the field next to the hospital to eat grass. Dr. Richardson or Peter would hold his lead rope while he grazed. The grass was so green and lush, he ate it like a

★ ★ ★ ★ ★ ★ ★ ★ ★ ★ ★ ★ ★ ★

lawn mower set on racing speed. If he tried to rear and buck, feeling so good, Dr. Richardson or Peter would pull him down and warn him, "Cut it out, now, big guy. You have to wait."

No risks could be taken. He'd come so far. *Oh well, oh well,* Barbaro seemed to say. Eating was what he really cared about most, anyway.

Every day the bandages on his back left leg were changed. Sometimes all his human friends took turns doing this—caretakers from the training farm, Peter, Michael Matz, along with the nurses at the hospital. Gretchen brought him buckets of grass she'd pulled out of her yard at home. One of her cats, a big yellow one, accidentally broke its leg, and she carried him around with a cast on his leg just as she wished she could carry Barbaro.

How lucky can a horse get?

In the fall the cast on his broken leg was taken off. The leg had healed very well. In fact, amazingly well. Barbaro's treatment was leaving new lessons in every treatment book. All he needed was a new hoof on his left hind leg and he'd be good to go.

Well, maybe not as good to go as before. But good all the same.

He couldn't say it, but everyone wished it for him— that one day he would live his life as just any ordinary

★   ★   ★   ★   ★   ★   ★   ★   ★   ★   ★   ★   ★

horse. Soon he would turn four. In the future he hoped to have lots of little Barbaros running around, the way he and Last Best Place used to run.

Back in Kentucky, Barbaro's mother, La Ville Rouge, was expecting her fifth baby in the spring of 2007. Last Best Place was on the East Coast in New York state. He had recently won his first big race. Still not very big, but as tough as ever, he was galloping his heart out down the homestretches of racetracks from New York to New Jersey. And no doubt he sometimes saw a horse that made him think, for a moment, that he was seeing his old friend Barbaro.

The staff at the hospital at New Bolton Center in Pennsylvania never got used to the outpouring of love and well wishes. Every day baskets and cards arrived for their most famous patient. The nation became caught up in the story of the famous athlete who exchanged his courage on the racetrack for the courage to hold on to his life. America adopted him as a new hero. The way Barbaro lived with uncertainty inspired thousands to do the same. His fans had claimed him. And he now belonged to the world.

Anytime anyone needed to be reminded of the power of love, they needed only to think of Barbaro. Some say animals bring out the best in us. If Barbaro could communicate in a language with letters and signs,

★　★　★　★　★　★　★　★　★　★　★　★　★　★

BARBARO: AMERICA'S HORSE   ★   125

he most likely would communicate his agreement. But for sure he would tack on a message:

> Whatever, whatever.
> And oh yeah, thanks!
> Thanks bunches.
> And please pass the sweet feed.

★ ★ ★ ★ ★ ★ ★ ★ ★ ★ ★ ★ ★ ★ ★

Afterword

EARLY IN 2007 BARBARO'S DOCTORS
and caretakers decided he no longer needed
the specialized care of the Intensive Care
Unit. Plans were being made to move him to
a Thoroughbred farm in Kentucky, where
horsemen are trained to care for racehorses
recovering from serious injury as well as
laminitis. A cast was placed on his left
hind leg to give it support for the trip and
to help realign a bone. But on January 9,
he suffered a setback when doctors found
new separation on the inside portion of
that left hind hoof. The diseased tissue was
removed, and once again Barbaro faced a
long wait for more hoof to grow.

All of us who saw Barbaro as a hero
who faced uncertainty with grace imagined
him living out his days in Kentucky,
grazing in knee-high blue grass, nickering
at fillies as they walked by. An added hope
was that his back legs would grow strong

★ ★ ★ ★ ★ ★ ★ ★ ★ ★ ★ ★

enough for him to pass his magnificent genes on to a new generation of champions.

But in the last week of January, Barbaro suffered yet another serious complication when he developed a deep abscess in his right hind foot. Surgery was performed to put a skeleton of pins, bars, and a plate around the leg—forming a brace—to take all the weight off the fragile bone structure. On January 28, Barbaro was ingeniously figuring out how to get around with his new contraption. And his eyes were bright.

Sir Thomas Browne wrote in 1886, "Life is pure flame, and we live by an invisible sun within us." That sun, however, rose in a different way early on the morning of January 29, when laminitis was found in both of Barbaro's front feet. Now even the light in Barbaro's eye told his owners, and all who loved him, that it was time to let him go. And they kindly gave permission to release their dear Barbaro to the green pastures beside the still waters. America's Barbaro was now a legend.

★ ★ ★ ★ ★ ★ ★ ★ ★ ★ ★ ★ ★ ★

Glossary

ABSCESS ★ A collection of pus. A horse will often have an abscess in a foot, and this is usually caused by pressure or a foreign object—that is, by a rock or something else that is not supposed to be there. The word "abscess" comes from a Latin word used in ancient Rome that means "to go away." Pus is the body's attempt to wash something away.

ALPACA ★ A South American mammal. A mammal is an animal whose babies are born alive—that is, not from an egg that hatches. And mammals' babies drink milk. An alpaca's hair is long and silky and is used to make cloth. An alpaca bleats, meaning it makes a sound like a sheep. And when an alpaca is angry or frightened, it spits!

ANESTHESIA ★ A chemical that can make an animal go into a deep sleep

★ ★ ★ ★ ★ ★ ★ ★ ★ ★ ★ ★

and lose consciousness so it cannot feel pain. The word "anesthesia" comes from an ancient Greek word meaning "without being able to feel."

BAY ★   This word can refer to a reddish brown color, or it can refer to a horse with a reddish brown body and a black mane and tail. The word comes from a Latin word that was the name of a color.

BLEMISH ★   A flaw that keeps something from being perfect. The word "blemish" comes from an old French word meaning "to make pale." In the horse world a blemish means a lump or scar. It may be unsightly, but it does not keep the horse from being sound. The horse is still fit for strenuous work.

BONDING ★   The love or affection between two animals. The word comes from an old English word meaning "band." Bonding among herd animals gives protection. Bonding between mother and baby provides safety. Bonding helps the baby survive.

BREEZING ★   A horseracing term meaning to let a horse run at a speed fast enough that the horse has to work really hard. Horsemen in the sport of racing explain breezing as a speed requiring a horse to exert itself.

★ ★ ★ ★ ★ ★ ★ ★ ★ ★ ★ ★ ★ ★

CANNON BONE ★ The large bone in a horse's leg. The splint bone is next to it and the coffin bone is under it in the hoof. An injury to the cannon bone is very serious, since this bone supports the horse's weight. An injury to the splint bone is most often unimportant because the splint bone does not bear weight. The coffin bone is the bone that can sink into the hoof when a horse founders or gets laminitis, which is a very serious, life-threatening condition.

CILIA ★ Cilia are like hair and can often move in a rhythm. The word "cilia" comes from a Latin word meaning "eyelid." Eyelashes are cilia. The pathways into the lungs have cilia to sweep them clean.

COLT ★ A young male horse that has not been neutered, so he can still have babies. A gelding is a male horse that has been neutered so he cannot have babies. A colt is called a stallion as he gets older and matures. Usually by the age of five all colts are called stallions. The word "colt" comes from an ancient Swedish word meaning "half-grown animal."

CONTAGIOUS DISEASE ★ A sickness that can be spread easily, such as by touching. The word "contagious" comes from an ancient Latin word meaning "to have contact with."

★ ★ ★ ★ ★ ★ ★ ★ ★ ★ ★ ★

DAM ★   The mother of an animal, such as a horse. The word "dam" comes from an English word that means "lady."

EOHIPPUS ★   The extinct animal that is the ancestor of the modern-day horse. It lived more than fifty million years ago in an age called the Eocene. It had four toes on each front foot, three toes on each back foot, and was about the size of a fox. The horse eventually got taller over many generations and was able to eat from trees as well as grass from the ground. These changes allowed it to survive.

EQUINE SURGEON ★   A doctor who operates on horses. An equine surgeon graduates from high school, goes through four years of college and four years of veterinary school, and then does three years of training as a surgeon. "Equine" is a word that comes from the Latin word "equus," which means "horse."

FARMER'S ALMANAC ★   A book published each year that contains calendars with the times when the sun and the moon rise and set, weather forecasts, and other useful information. Farmers consult the almanac to guide them in planting seeds. You can make your own almanac by collecting how many days

★ ★ ★ ★ ★ ★ ★ ★ ★ ★ ★ ★ ★ ★

of rain were in a month, the scores of ball games, the birthdays of family members and pets, and the books and movies most popular in a year. One of the most famous American almanacs was called *Poor Richard's Almanack*, written by Benjamin Franklin, one of the signers of the Declaration of Independence.

FILLY ★ A young female horse before she has a foal. After a filly is about four years old, she is called a "mare."

FLEHMEN ★ A behavioral response in which a horse opens its mouth and curls up its lip, making it look as though it is smiling. Actually, though, when a horse does this, it is trying to get a better sense of smell by using the sensitive skin on the inside of its lips. A horse most often uses a flehmen response when it smells something unusual for the first time.

FURLONG ★ A horseracing term meaning one eighth of a mile, or 220 yards. The word "furlong" grew from the description of a long furrow, which is the row plowed by a farmer.

INSTINCTS ★ Behaviors that help animals survive. They are not learned but are present from the moment of birth. Without fear, prey animals would be easy targets

★ ★ ★ ★ ★ ★ ★ ★ ★ ★ ★ ★

for predators, which would kill them for food. Horses are vegetarians, which means they do not eat meat. Horses fear meat-eating animals such as tigers and wolves. The horse's main instinct is to run from these predators. Other vegetarian animals, such as deer and cows, do not set off survival alarms within a horse. The word "instinct" comes from an ancient Latin word that means "to urge on."

LAMINITIS ★ Inflammation of the sensitive laminae inside the hooves. Laminae is tissue, like the skin cells underneath human fingernails. During an attack of laminitis, the laminae begin to tear loose from the rest of the hoof, and the coffin bone (the bottom bone of the foot) may sink down, making it very painful for a horse to bear weight. A horse that has had laminitis is said to be "foundered." There are many causes of laminitis; in Barbaro's case, his laminitis developed from the stress of his left hind leg bearing so much weight due to his broken right leg.

LIGAMENT ★ A tough band of tissue connecting two or more bones. The word "ligament" comes from a Latin word, "*ligare*," meaning "to bind."

LONG LINES ★ Reins attached to a horse's bridle so that the horse acts as though it is pulling a cart or

★ ★ ★ ★ ★ ★ ★ ★ ★ ★ ★ ★ ★

wagon when it is really only walking in front of a person. "Long lining" is a way to train a young horse to read the signals sent through reins. This exercise also strengthens a horse's hindquarters.

LUNGE LINE ★ A rope or long rein that is attached to a horse's halter or bridle so the horse can move in a circle around the person holding the lunge line. This exercise is said to be "lungeing" a horse.

NEIGH ★ One of the sounds a horse makes. A horse can neigh, nicker, and whinny as well as snort and squeal. A nicker is a low soft sound usually of greeting. A horse nickers when it sees feed coming. It neighs or whinnies when it calls to another horse. Horses cannot whimper or cry. The way they show that they are in pain is by kicking, rolling, dropping their heads with limp or flattened ears, and having dull eyes.

REGURGITATE ★ To cause to pour back, to vomit. "Regurgitate" comes from a Latin word, "*gurges,*" meaning "whirlpool."

SIRE ★ The father of an animal, such as a horse. The word "sire" comes from an old French word meaning "older."

★ ★ ★ ★ ★ ★ ★ ★ ★ ★ ★ ★

TWO-MINUTE LICK ★ (also written as "2' lick") A racehorse term meaning to run the equivalent of one mile in two minutes, or one eighth of a mile in fifteen seconds.

UMBILICAL CORD ★ An umbilical cord connects an unborn baby inside its mother with what it needs from the outside world, such as air and nourishment. It also takes away waste. It is a tube that connects to the baby's navel. The phrase "umbilical cord" is often used to describe any life-giving tool. For example, astronauts call the line that brings them oxygen an umbilical cord.

VETERINARIAN ★ A doctor who treats animals. Because there are fewer than thirty schools of veterinary medicine in the United States, students have to be very well prepared to be accepted into a veterinary school. Then a student has to be very focused to finish the four years of training.

WEAN ★ To separate a baby from its mother so it will no longer drink her milk. The word "wean" comes from an old English word meaning "to train."

YEARLING ★ A one-year-old horse.

★ ★ ★ ★ ★ ★ ★ ★ ★ ★ ★ ★ ★

Suggestions for Further Reading

BOOKS FOR ADULTS:

The Ten Trusts: What We Must Do to Care for the Animals We Love, by Jane Goodall and Marc Bekoff

When Elephants Weep: The Emotional Lives of Animals, by Jeffrey Moussaieff Masson and Susan McCarthy

Minding Animals: Awareness, Emotions, and Heart, by Marc Bekoff

The Smile of a Dolphin: Remarkable Accounts of Animal Emotions, edited by Marc Bekoff

The Nature of Horses: Exploring Equine Evolution, Intelligence, and Behavior, by Stephen Budiansky

The Equid Ethogram: A Practical Field Guide to Horse Behavior, by Sue McDonnell

★ ★ ★ ★ ★ ★ ★ ★ ★ ★ ★ ★ ★

RELATED WEBSITES:

www.janegoodall.org
www.equineresearch.org
www.pbs.org/wnet/nature/animalmind/emotion.html

CHILDREN'S BOOKS:

Animal Masterminds: A Chapter Book (True Tales), by Catherine
    Nichols

Animal Homes, by Ann O. Squire

Animal Babies, by Ann O. Squire

Tough Beginnings: How Baby Animals Survive, by Marilyn
    Singer and Anna Vojtech

The Burgess Animal Book for Children, by Thornton W.
    Burgess

Los Animales Hacen Cosas Asombrosas / Amazing Animal Behavior,
    by Susan McGrath, Pedro L. Aznar (adapter), and
    Maria T. Sanz (translator)

The Big Book of Amazing Animal Behavior, by Annette Tison
    and Talus Taylor

Strange Dances and Long Flights: A Book About Animal Behaviors,
    by Patricia M. Stockland and Todd Ouren

Animal Runners, by Kenneth Lilly (a board book for very
    young children)

★ ★ ★ ★ ★ ★ ★ ★ ★ ★ ★ ★ ★ ★

Letters to Barbaro

OVER THE MONTHS THAT BARBARO has been in the hospital, he has received thousands of messages and cards. Here are excerpts from a few Gretchen Jackson selected to share with you:

Dear Barbaro,
I think you're gonna be fine. God is with you always. My class and I are praying for you. . . . Everybody wants to help. God is gonna come through for you.

Sincerely,
Michael

Dear Barbaro and Michael Matz,
I hope you get better, Barbaro. You were my favorite horse. . . . Too bad you can't race again.
Tell Barbaro everything I said to him, Michael Matz. And you are one of the best trainers.

From,
Ross

★ ★ ★ ★ ★ ★ ★ ★ ★ ★ ★ ★

Dear Barbaro,

I hope you feel better soon. You are a good racing horse. I hope the vets are taking good care of you.

Love,

Steven, first grade

Dear Barbaro,

Hang in there. . . . We are praying for you. Our teacher has a horse farm and loves horses. Get well soon. You have a 50-50 chance, which is pretty good for a horse who broke his ankle. Meet the challenge, Barbaro.

Sincerely,

Laura

Dear Dr. Dean,

I hope you will help heal Barbaro's leg so he can walk again.

By:

Kendall

Dear Barbaro,

I hope your leg is feeling better! Even though you can't win the Triple Crown, your run in the Derby was amazing! You had an awesome racing

★ ★ ★ ★ ★ ★ ★ ★ ★ ★ ★ ★ ★

career and always made coming in first place look easy. Go, Barbaro!

—*Lauren*

Dear Barbaro,
I hope you get better. And here's a picture I drew of you in the starting gate.

Love,
Schaefer

Dear Barbaro,
I hope your leg feels better and that you will still be a legend and that you will be still alive for me to see you one day.

From,
Nicholas

Dear Barbaro,
I hope your ankle will get well. You're a great horse. Here's a picture of carrots, apples, grain, and sugar cubes and lots of other treats.

Sincerely,
Quinn

Dear Barbaro,
Get well. Happy carrots to you.

From a fan

★ ★ ★ ★ ★ ★ ★ ★ ★ ★ ★ ★ ★ ★

Dear Barbaro,
Today in school we made get-well cards for you. Hopefully, they will make you and the people who take care of you feel better.

Our school is close to your home racetrack and our teacher lives close to the hospital that is taking care of you. We all hope you feel better soon.

We love you.
All Miss Z's kindergarten students

Dear Barbaro,
We love you. We hope you get better real soon. You are amazing and you will always be remembered.

Rachael, 11

Dear Barbaro,
You are the bravest horse ever. When I grow up I want to be a veterinarian so I can help animals like you. . . . Get well soon, sweet stuff!

Haley, 7

★ ★ ★ ★ ★ ★ ★ ★ ★ ★ ★ ★ ★

Dear Barbaro,

I LOVE YOU SO MUCH. I look forward to the update tomorrow cuz I want to know how you are doing! Stay strong 4 ever!!!

Much love,
Colleen, 16

Dear Barbaro,

You have helped me a lot. Before the Preakness, I was just a girl who was hard and NEVER cried about anything. I didn't have the softy in me. After the race, I've been bawling over many things that I have wanted to cry about for so long and could not. I figured if Edgar Prado, the famous, tough, handsome, never-say-die jockey could cry, then so could I! Now, even though I am not what you'd call a "girlie girl," I have found a heart for others.

Thank you, and thank God for helping you through.

Your numero uno fan,
Cheri, 14

P.S. Who is your little bro and is he going to race in the Triple Crown?

★ ★ ★ ★ ★ ★ ★ ★ ★ ★ ★ ★ ★ ★

Mr. and Mrs. Roy Jackson,

Every year my second-grade class watches and keeps records of the Triple Crown races. We learn about measurement, probability, and distance. This year we learned about courage and depth of feeling.

The important lesson we have taken away from this splendid horse is that good people, like you, don't give up. And that strangers, like my class and Barbaro, can be linked forever by a frightening event. You and your fine horse are in our daily morning prayers.

Deborah, second-grade teacher

★ ★ ★ ★ ★ ★ ★ ★ ★ ★ ★ ★ ★ ★

Acknowledgments

ONE DAY MARK AMBRECHT, THE farrier who was helping me keep my dear horse Skip going in his fight against laminitis, turned to me and said, "You know, that story of Barbaro has all the parts of how love can heal a horse." I didn't know anything about the sport of racing, but I sure knew about the bond between a horse and someone who loves him. It was then that, as a writer of adult novels for more than forty years, I switched gears and took off on the trail of the story of Barbaro. Instinctively I knew the story was meant for children, especially those who, like myself, were born with the horse-love chromosome.

Without these dedicated people whose lives became so completely entwined with the great Barbaro, this story would never have taken flight—Gretchen and Roy

★ ★ ★ ★ ★ ★ ★ ★ ★ ★ ★ ★

Jackson, who shared Barbaro with me and became dear friends. Peter Brette, who was perhaps closer to Barbaro than anyone else, gave me his cell phone number and joined up in helping me feel the story. On occasion Peter answered my phone calls while holding Barbaro as he grazed in the field behind New Bolton Center. And together we relived certain moments in Barbaro's life.

Michael Matz kindly spent a whole day with me, letting me feel the flow of his training farm and letting me crawl inside a few minds there. Dr. Kathy Anderson gave me many insights into what Barbaro experienced en route to the hospital. The staff at Fair Hill Training Center were especially helpful—Sue Danner, Tammy Burlin, Bertha Turnbull, Fenneka Bentley, Emily Daignault. Teresa Ferris's photographs caught many of Barbaro's days there.

As for the beginning of the story, it never would have gotten off the ground without Bill Sanborn and his wife, Sandy, who helped me see the day Barbaro was born and also Barbaro's amazing friendship with Last Best Place. John and Jill Stephens are among the best horse trainers I've ever seen and generously gave me the story of Barbaro as a yearling. The day I spent following Jill around will stay in my memory as one of my most joyous days, forever.

Lisa Whitcomb, who runs interference for the

Jackson family, kindly cleared the way for me, and Julia
Richardson at Simon & Schuster was the bestest with the
mostest, getting this story off and soaring, while Ellen
Krieger and Liesa Abrams superbly brought it down the
homestretch.

Here at home, friends were spectacular in their
support—Julian and Diane Cotter, Chris Machen, Dale
Kaplan-Stein, Marilyn McLean, and vets, Drs. Eleanor
Green and Susan Tannhauser. My own family never
falters in their support of my writing habit—Parker,
my love; my kids, Blake and Paul; and their families:
Brian, Bryce, and Lindsey. And thanks to my own horses
who every day remind me that they are horses and I'm
only a lowly pencil-holding human hanging on: Mullet,
Precious, and of course Skip, who also taught me to let
him go to the greener pastures beside the still waters,
where he lives on in memory.

★ ★ ★ ★ ★ ★ ★ ★ ★ ★ ★ ★ ★ ★ ★